THE FREEMASONIC PLOT
TO DESTROY THE CHURCH

THE
VIRGIN
AND THE
PENTACLE

ALAN BUTLER

Copyright © 2005 O Books
O Books is an imprint of The Bothy, John Hunt Publishing Ltd.,
Deershot Lodge, Park Lane, Ropley, Hants, SO24 0BE, UK
office@johnhunt-publishing.com
www.O-books.net

Distribution in:
UK
Orca Book Services
orders@orcabookservices.co.uk
Tel: 01202 665432 Fax: 01202 666219 Int. code (44)

USA and Canada
NBN
custserv@nbnbooks.com
Tel: 1 800 462 6420 Fax: 1 800 338 4550

Australia
Brumby Books
sales@brumbybooks.com
Tel: 61 3 9761 5535 Fax: 61 3 9761 7095

New Zealand
Peaceful Living
books@peaceful-living.co.nz
Tel: 64 7 57 18105 Fax: 64 7 57 18513

Singapore
STP
davidbuckland@tlp.com.sg
Tel: 65 6276 Fax: 65 6276 7119

South Africa
Alternative Books
altbook@global.co.za
Tel: 27 011 792 7730 Fax: 27 011 972 7787

Text: © compiler Alan Butler 2005

Design: BookDesign™, London

ISBN 1 905047 32 0

A CIP catalogue record for this book is available from the British
Library.

Printed in the USA by Maple-Vail Manufacturing Group

THE FREEMASONIC PLOT
TO DESTROY THE CHURCH

THE
VIRGIN
AND THE
PENTACLE

ALAN BUTLER

BOOKS

WINCHESTER UK
NEW YORK USA

CONTENTS

Introduction   vii

Chapter 1   A Vision on the Mountain   2

Chapter 2   The Aftermath   10

Chapter 3   Stranger and Stranger   24

Chapter 4   Inside the Lodge   32

Chapter 5   The Weeping Virgin   42

Chapter 6   Into the Melting Pot   52

Chapter 7   The Quiet Revolution   60

Chapter 8   The Jerusalem Connection   68

Chapter 9   From Templarism to Freemasonry   78

Chapter 10   The Cult of Mary   88

Chapter 11   Freemasonry and the Rise of Science   100

Chapter 12   The Seeds of Revolution   108

Chapter 13   The Hidden Imperative   120

Chapter 14   The Alta Vendita   130

Chapter 15   The Pentacle – Darkness or Light   142

Chapter 16   London and the Goddess of Britain   160

Chapter 17   An Epilogue to a Vision   174

Appendix   183

Index   187

INTRODUCTION

INTRODUCTION

History is not always what it seems to be. To a certain extent it is the creation of historians themselves. It has to be; much of the truth underpinning specific events has been lost in the mists of time and assumptions are inevitable. We tend to glide over these mysteries of the past. It is these mysteries that have fascinated me since childhood.

A good example of this is the existence of pyramids all over the world. Pyramids of one sort or another are to be found not only in Egypt, but also in Asia, as well as in North, Central, and South America. There appears to be no logical connection between these structures, built at different times by cultures that do not seem to have been directly associated. Of course, there are only a limited number of ways of putting stones together to gain height. But what drew these diverse cultures to build these astonishing monuments in the first place? Many observers have suggested that there was a much greater degree of world travel and cross-fertilization of ideas in prehistory than we have so far recognized. Some people go further. "Maybe," they suggest, "historians do know much more about this situation than they are willing to admit. Perhaps there is some agenda at work here, deliberately fostered to keep ordinary people ignorant of the real truths from history." Thus a conspiracy theory is born, of which there are many thousands in the world today.

During the long period in which I have been fascinated by history, I must have come across just about every conspiracy theory that has ever been proposed. Was the earth seeded with life by a bunch of well-meaning aliens from some far distant part of space? Is it possible that there was once a super-civilization, the existence of which we can infer but never fully prove? Did the Egyptians have access to advanced technology when they erected the Great Pyramid of over three and a half million heavy stones? And most important of all – are there people alive today who know the answer to all of this but who are deliberately keeping their knowledge secret?

One by one I have looked at people's ideas about the mysteries that are relevant to history and I have traveled extensively in order to try and corroborate facts at first hand. I was and remain skeptical about conspiracy theories generally, but against my better judgement I came to discover, slowly but surely, that there has been and still is one powerful and enduring conspiracy in our world. This emanates from a period at least five millennia ago but has been specifically important to the development of the world during the last thousand years.

There is no ambiguity about this particular conspiracy because its effects are felt in all our lives on each passing day. Neither does one have to look very far in order to see evidence of its existence. It can be observed almost everywhere. For example, step into any average Catholic Church, or stand on board a ship entering New York Harbor in the United States and you will view the conspiracy at first hand. Walk into a bank anywhere in the world and withdraw cash from your account or cast your vote in a local or national election and you are participating in the conspiracy yourself.

The conspiracy in question is present in capitalism, in democracy, in freedom of speech – in fact just about everywhere and in everything we take for granted. It is to be found in the square mile of London, known as "the City," and in Time Square in New York. It was at work when a bunch of armed fanatics attacked the Holy Land in 1099 and it was still evident when a group of men came together to pen the words of the United States Constitution. For good or ill it moved tens of thousands of people off the land and into cities during the seventeenth and eighteenth centuries in Britain and Ireland. It inspired technology, the rise of science, universal education, transport systems, international trade, and world travel.

At the heart of this quite genuine conspiracy lies a constant and ongoing war that has taken place since a long-dead Roman Emperor initiated a meeting in Anatolia in the year AD 325. The struggle has been between two quite distinct groups of people with very different ideas about how religion and society should be run. One of these groups is known to us all – in the last couple of millennia it has been called the Christian Church. The other group is harder to pin down, despite the fact that we owe just about everything we presently are to its enduring influence.

Those of us who were, like me, brought up amidst Western Christianity, were taught to believe that it was the influence of Christianity and the Fathers of the Church that brought us out of the Dark Ages. It was thanks to the Church that tyranny had eventually been overthrown and a civilizing hand spread across the world. But this is simply not the case. The people who were brought up for generations to pass on this myth were themselves hoodwinked.

The truth of the matter is that, left to its own devices, Christianity – or rather the people who ran it – would have been quite happy if most of us were still leaving our squalid hovels each day to harness a yoke of oxen we didn't own and to plough land over which we had no control, trapped in a life of ignorance and servitude. The Church didn't care that we were illiterate, innumerate or impoverished, just as long as we did what we were told. Orthodox Christianity was a tool of a repressive feudal society that had to be dragged, kicking and screaming, all the way to the twenty-first century and the leaders of the Church are still trying to run the world. The people who made the changes possible were the conspirators. They fought Christian feudalism from within by infiltrating its very heart. They used just about any means at their disposal to undermine the combined forces of Church and State that had conspired for centuries to make us the tools of its own will.

Modern Western society is far from perfect. It has looked on blankly as millions starved in order that a minority can have what most of the world's population would consider to be a lavish lifestyle. More than this, it has exploited poorer nations for its own purposes and some say it is still doing so right now. Nevertheless, the fact remains that, slowly but surely, third world nations are catching up. It's a long and brutal struggle but democracy is winning as more and more people have the right to choose their own forms of government and free themselves from tyranny and slavery.

Each of us is now more "aware" of what is going on around our planet than has ever been the case before. People – millions of people – rally and demonstrate regularly, without any hope of personal gain, to assist others who live thousands of miles distant. When raw nature strikes one section of the world's population, their fellows, continents away, raise billions of dollars to help out. Love it or loathe it this is the legacy of capitalism and democracy. Without the conspiracy we would not have either.

If all of this sounds too fantastic to be true, then join the club. For many years as my research continued I told myself that the subversion of whole societies, across so many centuries, could not have been possible, at least not without all of us being quite aware of what has gone on. In reality our ignorance has been made possible because of a host of different factors. For starters, the people responsible do not advertise their presence through political parties. They have not written slogans on banners or, except very rarely, fought wars to gain their objectives. They have simply "leaned on" society, subtly, repeatedly, and relentlessly. They work from within existing institutions, even the established Church itself, and have created others that have been used as conduits – moving from sphere to sphere and place to place, in order to gradually remold the shape of society. When a particular organization or institution became lax or no longer served its original purpose it was abandoned by the conspirators. All of this has been done in secret, and yet when we open our eyes there is really no secret at all.

Who then are these people, who for dozens of generations have been quietly working, chipping away at the foundations of dictatorship, slavery, and oppression? The truth is that as far as the modern world is concerned, they remain nameless because that is how they want things to be. We can guess who some of them are and we can certainly recognize their actions in the past. We can even put names to quite a few of the historical individuals concerned but if there is a central nucleus of conspirators still functioning in the world, they remain elusive and, to most of us, even invisible.

Perhaps the time has come to end this age-old secret. Maybe we have grown up enough to introduce ourselves to a very different way of thinking and acting that has been commonplace to one section of society, while the rest of us remained blissfully unaware. That is the purpose of this book. I will present the evidence as convincingly as I can, and then you can make up your own mind whether I am correct, or just another disillusioned soul with a quirky way of looking at history and the world.

I started to trip over these "changers of the world" many years ago when I began making connections in history that were quite clear, yet which should not have existed at all. And one factor shared by those who fell under my gaze was quite apparent. They had a reverence for the "feminine," especially within religion. The silent war to which society has been party for so long amounts to a battle between the Christian Church and a mysterious female deity who was worshiped for millennia before the Sermon on the Mount or the Last Supper even took place. Our conspirators are, quite simply, Goddess worshipers.

I eventually came to realize that the peculiar religious belief that is still plainly present at the heart of society exists alongside an insatiable desire for free will, equality, and fairness. And nowhere in the modern world is there a better home for these alternative beliefs than deep at the heart of an institution that is presently under attack from Catholics and Christian fundamentalists all over the world. I have come to realize that if we want to gain a true idea of who our conspirators actually are and have been, we can do no better than to look closely at Freemasonry and the organizations that led to its existence.

What follows is a story that will take us back many thousands of years but I want to begin by visiting a much more recent era. The date is 19 September 1846 and the location is a mountaintop above a small village in Eastern France.

CHAPTER ONE

A Vision on the Mountain

A VISION ON THE MOUNTAIN

It was 19 September 1846. In the East the first fingers of dawn were just discernible over the mountain peaks, illuminating the dazzling face of the planet Venus. Now at her very brightest Venus had risen over an hour before and was hovering a full twenty degrees above the horizon. The trio of people, following a small herd of sleepy cattle and a couple of bleating goats, shambled out of the little hamlet of Ablandins, setting their sights on the hill pastures that stretched away before them towards the peak of La Salette.

Out in front, with his scythe over his shoulder, was the farmer, Pierre Selme, bound for a day cutting hay – winter fodder for his beasts. Next came Melanie Calvet,[1] fourteen years old but small for her age. She wore a long, full, homespun dress that reached down to her boots. Above this she sported a pinafore, as was the local tradition, and a lace cap tied under her chin completed the ensemble. With sleep still on her mind Melanie was no doubt quiet on that beautiful September morning, but there was nothing unusual about that.

Bringing up the rear, swinging his stout stick and playing games with his little dog Loulou, was Maximin Giraud. He was even smaller than Melanie, some said more like an eight-year-old despite his eleven years, but big enough and old enough for work in the pastoral setting of South West France in the year 1846. He wasn't a professional cowherd, as Melanie had already been for a number of years. His father had been prevailed upon to let his son come from his hometown of Corps, some miles distant, to look after the cattle and goats of Farmer Selme, whilst his usual shepherd was away sick.

Both the children were from a grindlingly poor background. The meager wages they could earn for keeping the cattle safe from wandering too near to the many sheer drops on the mountainside would be welcome to supplement pitifully small family incomes. Neither had known any real schooling. They were illiterate and did not even have much French, speaking, as did most of their contemporaries, a local patois. Not that Melanie spoke much at all. She was a brooding and often sullen child, bitten from infancy by the ravages of poverty: poorly clothed, poorly fed, and often ignored.

---

1 Melanie also used the surname Mathieu, which seems to have been interchangeable with Calvet.

The steep slopes lay before them and soon the farmer turned to take a different track, trusting his precious cattle to the capricious Maximin, while Melanie was in charge of the livestock of another farmer, Baptiste Pra. It was a beautiful early autumn day and as the beasts arrived at their pasture, the silver face of Venus had already disappeared into the azure blue of day. The two children set about their usual routine, which wasn't exactly demanding. All that was required was to keep the cows safe and to drive them to water in the middle of the day. As a rule for Melanie it was a life of solitude, but that suited her fine – far better than being lumbered with the nervy, chattering Maximin, whose incessant banter disturbed her.

The day grew warmer and by the time the midday bell sounded from the little church down in the village below, the children were hungry and thirsty. Together, they drove the cattle down a little way to a place where a natural spring broke the surface of the meadow. There, while the animals drank their fill, the children ate their meager lunch of bread and cheese, washed down with nothing more appealing than water. Other herders joined them for a short while before wandering off to attend to their own tasks and, laying down in the course meadow grass, Melanie and her young companion soon fell asleep under the midday sun.

Some two hours later they awoke, Melanie getting up quickly, her practiced eyes searching for her charges. She was alarmed to see that they had wandered close to the edge of a ravine some way off. She quickly woke the still sleeping Maximin so that the cattle could be driven back to safer ground. Reaching the edge of the ravine ahead of her companion Melanie looked down to see what she later described as a great circle of light. Puzzled, she called to Maximin, who was running on behind her. The children were both alarmed and little Maximin, whose bravery outstripped his size, clung tenaciously to his stick, telling Melanie to do the same in case they should need to defend themselves. The shabby pair were transfixed as their eyes became accustomed to the light and the vision before them took on the shape of a beautiful woman. She was seated and bent slightly forward, and it soon became obvious that she was weeping quietly. Maximin said later that he had thought she might be a woman from one of the local villages who, having been beaten by her husband or mistreated by her family, had wandered to this solitary spot to cry alone. But it soon became obvious that this could not be the case because the form before them looked nothing like any woman they had ever seen before in the district. She wore a long white dress and a beautiful veil, topped by a wonderful crown. All around the base of the crown were roses of red and white, which were repeated on the shawl around her shoulders. Tied around her waist the children saw that she sported a large yellow apron, which glistened as if it was made of gold. On her feet she wore white slippers, also bedecked with roses and clusters of pearls. Around the neck of the stunningly beautiful woman hung a crucifix, wrought in gold or shining bronze. The figure on the cross seemed to burn like fire and the jewel also sported a small hammer and a pair of pliers to either side of the cross; as Melanie commented later, the tools used to fasten Jesus to the cross and to remove him after his death.

The vision now spoke, in a voice that was gentle and calm. She still wept but stood and encouraged the children to approach her. "Come to me my children," she instructed. "Do not be afraid. I am here to tell you something of the greatest importance."

Scrambling down the sides of the ravine the children crossed the small stream at its base and approached the now smiling woman. She spoke again and by now the children were so close they could have reached out and touched her.

If my people do not obey, I shall be compelled to loose my Son's arm. It is so heavy, so pressing that I can no longer restrain it. How long have I suffered for you! If my Son is not to cast you off, I am obliged to entreat Him without ceasing. But you take no least heed of that. No matter how well you pray in future, no matter how well you act, you will never be able to make up to me what I have endured on your behalf.

If occurred to Melanie that the wonderful, queenly woman was talking to them in French, a language with which she had only a rudimentary familiarity, and yet she understood. More words followed:

I have appointed you six days for working. The seventh I have reserved for myself. And no one will give it to me. This it is which causes the weight of my Son's arm to be so crushing.

The cart drivers cannot swear without bringing in my Son's name. These are the two things which make my Son's arm so burdensome.

The children listened transfixed as the message continued:

If the harvest is spoiled, it is your own fault. I warned you last year by means of the potatoes. You paid no attention. Quite the reverse, when you discovered that the potatoes had decayed, you swore, you abused my Son's name. They will continue to be spoiled, and by Christmas time this year there will be none left.

The children must have looked quizzically at each other and the woman seemed to take this as a lack of understanding on their part. "Ah, you do not understand French my children. Well then listen. I shall put it differently." The mysterious stranger now began to talk in the same patois that was the children's everyday speech. She continued:

> If you have grain, it will do no good to sow it, for what you sow the beasts will eat and whatever part of it springs up will crumble into dust when you thresh it.
>
> A great famine is coming. But before that happens the children under seven years of age will be seized with trembling and die in the arms of the parents holding them. The grown-ups will pay for their sins by hunger. The grapes will rot and the walnuts will turn bad.

The apparition now turned its attention specifically to Maximin and, although she spoke to him at length, Melanie reported afterwards that she could not catch a single word of what was said. She put this down to the fact that a secret had been told to the young lad that wasn't for anyone else to hear. After a while it was Melanie's turn to be addressed directly and she received what was to become the most important message imparted on that day at La Salette, though the content of the message would not be made public for many years.

The woman now addressed both children again, saying, "If people are converted, the rocks will become piles of wheat and it will be found that the potatoes have sown themselves." She was quiet for a while, as if leaving time for the words to sink in, but then she continued again, looking pointedly at the children: "Do you say your prayers well, my children?" Maximin quite honestly admitted that he at least did not. The woman looked disappointed. "Ah, my children," she continued, "it is very important to do so, at night and in the morning. When you don't have time, at least say an Our Father and a Hail Mary, and when you can, say more."

The vision then went on to complain that only a few very old women attended Mass in these sinful days and that hardly anyone took any notice of Lent, going, as she said, "to the butcher's shop like dogs." She asked the children if they had ever seen spoiled wheat? The ever-gregarious Maximin was the first so speak up again, declaring that he'd never seen such a thing.

> But you, my child, you must have seen it once, near Coin, with your papa. The owner of a field said to your papa, "Come and see my spoiled wheat."

The two of you went. You took two or three ears of wheat in your hands. You rubbed them and they crumbled to dust. Then you came back from Coin. When you were only a half-hour away from Corps, your papa gave you a bit of bread and said. "Well, my son, eat some bread this year, anyhow. I don't know who'll be eating any next year if the wheat continues to spoil like that."

With great disbelief at this apparent re-telling of an incident he'd all but forgotten himself, Maximin said, "It's very true, Madame. Now I remember it. Until now I didn't."

Now the shining lady spoke for the last time, again in French. "Well my children," she instructed, "you will make this known to my people." She then turned and stepped over the almost-dry streambed. Transfixed, they watched as she walked the full length of the ravine. The children followed her at least part of the way and they noticed that for the first time since she had appeared, she had ceased crying. When she was some distance away the light by which she had been surrounded at her appearance began to shine brightly again and then she gradually disappeared into the full glow of the afternoon.

The children remained transfixed for some time. With no more than a rudimentary understanding of the Christian religion, into which she had been born but barely instructed, Melanie breathlessly commented that perhaps the lady had been a great saint. Little Maximin agreed and suggested that had they known they were in the presence of a saint, perhaps they could have prevailed upon her to take them with her – to wherever she had gone. Melanie then said something that might well prove very telling when the time for an inquest arrived: "She did not want us to watch her any longer, so that we could not see where she went."

Within half an hour, the cattle were watered once more. Their meager possessions gathered together the children began to drive the livestock home again, down the gentle slopes to the hamlet. As they began walking through the springy grass Maximin asked Melanie what the beautiful lady had said specifically to her.

"She did tell me something," Melanie confirmed, but then added, "But I shan't tell it to you. She told me not to." Doubtless Maximin sulked a little but threw off her remark by saying, "Well that doesn't bother me. She told me something too, and I'm not going to tell you either."

It occurred to the children as they tried to urge their reluctant charges away from the lush grass and down towards Ablandins, that the whole place would most certainly be a buzz of excitement. In their wildest dreams they could not envisage that they alone would be the recipients of such a vision. How disappointed they must have been to find the streets deserted and nobody running here and there, excitedly commenting on such monumental events. After all it isn't every day that a small and remote place like Ablandins could claim the visit of a saint.

When Maximin left Melanie and took his livestock along the village road, he arrived home to find farmer Selme waiting impatiently for him. Selme had returned from his hay cutting some time earlier and was anxious about his cattle. He didn't have a lot of respect for Maximin's abilities as a shepherd and demanded to know why the boy was so late. Maximin told the truth and explained that they would have been back earlier, had it not been for the fact that they had been delayed by the mysterious woman that they had seen in the ravine. Selme was skeptical to say the least and demanded a fuller explanation. Young Maximin retold the events on La Salette to the best of his abilities but Selme merely thought that the lad was lying in order to escape his wrath over the boy's dallying. But Maximin would give no ground and so it was decided that after they had eaten they would go to farmer Pra's house, to see whether Melanie would corroborate the young scamp's ridiculous story.

As it turned out Maximin didn't wait for his angry employer but immediately he had bolted down a few mouthfuls of food he rushed off to the Pra household. He burst into the house but Melanie was not there because she was still busy in the stable. The boy asked whether nobody in the Pra household had seen a beautiful lady surrounded by fire, who had passed through the air that afternoon.

As it happened the ever-secretive Melanie had said nothing, probably realizing better than her younger companion that her story would be immediately disbelieved. The adults seated around the table in the low kitchen listened with incredulity at the story young Maximin had to tell. Doubtless most of them scoffed, but the grandmother of the family, who had shown more kindness to Melanie than her younger relatives, rose from the table and went out to the stable to seek the girl.

She found Melanie tending to the cattle but obliged her to leave the beasts for the moment and to come into the house to corroborate Maximin's fantastic tale. Melanie was reluctant, saying that they had obviously already heard the story but after some prompting she followed the old woman back to the house. She was made to stand in the kitchen and tell the story all over again, probably in a more deliberate and detailed manner than the ever-jittery and excitable Maximin, but those present marveled immediately at how what she had to say conformed to what they had just heard.

Although neither of the children had the remotest idea about what they had actually seen on the mountain, Grandma Pra was in no doubt. She was one of the old ladies who had been alive before the torment, persecution, and social upheaval of the French Revolution and had retained a deep religious conviction vouchsafed to her since infancy. The same could not be said for the younger generation, who were often accused of being godless. She turned accusingly to her son. "Did you hear what the blessed Virgin said to this child? I suppose you will still be going out to work tomorrow – it's Sunday remember."

Her son was disbelieving and unrepentant, commenting that the Virgin Mary would hardly be likely to show herself to two urchin children who as far as he could see had shown no interest in religion whatsoever.

Did the words of Grandma Pra mean anything to Melanie or Maximin? Certainly they had made no suggestion that the woman they had seen up in the pasture was the Virgin Mary. It probably would not have occurred to them. Modern commentators on these events estimate that neither of the children can have gone to church often, if at all. Later in life Melanie claimed that she had been subjected to even earlier visions than this, but by that time she had become an embittered middle-aged woman, much at odds with the Church and the way it treated her. There doesn't seem to have been any recognition that there was anything special about her at the time.

It wasn't long before farmer Selme arrived, and very soon the small kitchen was crowded with other villagers. With each newcomer the children were made to rehearse their accounts all over again. Eventually the consensus was that here was an event beyond the experience of anyone present. There was nothing else for it but to take the whole story to the parish priest and see what he could make of it. But no priest was to be had at this time on a Saturday evening, so it was decided that he should be sought out ahead of morning Mass on the following day. For now the children should be put to bed.

Melanie was found in the now almost empty kitchen, on her knees and praying, as what now appeared to have been the Virgin Mary had told her to do. A look at Melanie Calvet's later life shows that she always had a flair for the dramatic and maybe this had already started. But she might well have prayed on that Saturday evening for both courage and patience because what she and her young companion Maximin Giraud were about to undergo would have made demands on the most resolute and confident person to be found in the length and breadth of France.

CHAPTER TWO

THE AFTERMATH

THE AFTERMATH

For some reason no adult accompanied the two children the next morning as they walked the short distance from Ablandins to the village of La Salette, where the priest lived. The only person they met on the way was the local constable. It was still short of 7am and he asked them where they were going. They replied that they had business with the priest but this only fired his curiosity and he demanded to know what that business might be.

After a few minutes he left the children in the road, laughing to himself at the story they had related. He was on his way to see the local mayor. Doubtless this would make an interesting diversion to the parish business that was at hand on that day.

Arriving at the rectory Melanie and Maximin went round to the back of the house and timidly knocked at the door. The priest's housekeeper answered their knock but refused to let them in to see the good father until they first told her the nature of their business. Once again they trotted out the story in full, while unbeknown to them Father Perrin, who was soon to be leaving the parish for another calling, was sitting as his desk in an adjoining room listening to every word. It is probably thanks to the immediate and very emotional response of this one individual on that Sunday morning in La Salette that knowledge of this vision is known to us even now.

When they had finished relating their story to the housekeeper the old man came into the kitchen. He had tears streaming down his face and it was obvious that he was already in no doubt whatsoever that the two little ragamuffins had genuinely encountered none other that the Blessed Virgin Mary herself. There was little time for discussion and the priest hurried across to the church to attend to morning Mass. Still highly emotional, he blurted out the story from his pulpit, to the absolute amazement of the few parishioners present. Maximin had been taken home to Corps, his duties as a shepherd now being over, but Melanie, who had attended the church service, now wandered home alone to the Pra household. A virtual volcano awaited her there.

The constable had told the mayor, an educated man by the name of Peytard, what he in turn had been told early in the day by the children. Peytard was nobody's fool. He does not seem to have been an unfair or unreasonable man, but he had been educated into the new ways of France, the ways of liberty, freed from what had often been seen as the tyrannical hold of the old Catholic Church back in the days of the Crown. He realized that if the parish constable knew the story, then just about everyone in the district would learn it soon enough and he took a conscious decision to nip this flower in the bud as quickly as possible. So it was that soon after Melanie arrived home, farmer Pra greeted the mayor cordially and offered him a drink. They talked for a while in the kitchen but it wasn't long before Melanie was sent for.

What followed was merely a curtain raiser for what Melanie and Maximin would both encounter during the next five years and beyond. Using every trick and device he could think of the mayor of La Salette did his best to dismiss Melanie's account of what had taken place the day before. When encouragement didn't work he used threats of arrest and imprisonment. Since this didn't achieve his objective any better he finally employed bribery, throwing fifteen francs onto the old kitchen table. He told Melanie the money would be hers if she admitted the story of the vision had been a fabrication. Fifteen franks probably represented at least three months' wages to Melanie but nevertheless she stood her ground. Nothing Peytard could say or do made the slightest difference. Melanie did not change any aspect of the story she had to tell and could not be tricked into stumbling over any part of it.

Meanwhile Maximin had arrived home in Corps, where he related the tale to his grandmother. His father, an inveterate drinker and ne'er do well, received the news in a local bar, where he was downing wine with his friends. He was teased unmercifully by the assembled boozers and determined to punish his son mightily when he got home. As it turned out he could not shake Maximin's conviction regarding what had happened on the previous day and in disgust he sent the lad to bed.

The community around Corps was small and insular. Not much happened in the district so when a story such as this broke, it shot down the lanes and among the thatched old cottages like wild fire. The parish priest ultimately responsible for both Melanie and Maximin in their hometown of Corps had heard the tale in full before the end of the day. His name was Father Mélin, a careful, just, and steady man. Being more than a simple parish priest he held the title of archpriest of the diocese and as such he had the ear of the local bishop. Despite the rumors that raced around the crowded streets of Corps he kept his council until the following Saturday, at which time he had established that Melanie Calvet would be coming home to see her parents. When she arrived he let it be known that he wanted to see the two children at his house immediately.

In his own quiet way he was as good an interrogator as the mayor and unlike Peytard he had access to both children. For several hours, separately and together, he grilled both Melanie and Maximin but could get no nearer to causing either of them to either recant or stumble than anyone else who had fired questions at them constantly since the previous weekend.

The story of the children's encounter simply would not go away. Already some forward-looking printer had produced a hastily drawn image of the apparition and this began to circulate in the district. Father Mélin therefore decided to get in touch with his bishop, a man by the name of de Bruillard, but before he did so he wanted to see the scene of the encounter for himself. So, on the following day, a small crocodile of people made their steady way up the flank of the mountain to the pasture. There, the ever-cautious Mélin insisted that the children told the whole story again, walking to the places in question and showing him specifically where the beautiful lady had appeared and disappeared. It was noticed at this time that the dried-up stream, which occupied the site of the happening, had suddenly started to flow again, which usually only happened after heavy rain or during the spring thaw. Quite mysteriously, for a man who supposedly had not yet made up his mind about the validity of the children's account, Father Mélin filled a bottle with the water and then returned to Corps.

Father Mélin's superior, Bishop de Bruillard, was as careful as Mélin himself, if not more so, and it was obvious from the outset that he would not make any premature judgement regarding the encounter at La Salette without undertaking a rigorous inquiry. In the end there were several different investigations by alternative religious and lay committees. At every stage the children were questioned just as vigorously as had been the case on the first day.

Quite soon Melanie and Maximin were famous and could hardly go anywhere without being virtually mobbed. The Church authorities recognized this fact and since the vision had not yet been full investigated, it was decided that the best thing would be to get the children out of harm's way. They were both sent to a local convent in Corps. Melanie would stay there but Maximin would attend on a daily basis. While they were there they would be educated at the expense of the parish and would be given at least some protection from the thronging mob.

Even though winter was gradually setting in, and despite the fact that the bishop had absolutely forbidden any of his priests from saying the remotest thing about the supposed vision, each day more and more people trudged through La Salette and up the mountain slope. On weekdays there were dozens but every Sunday the numbers swelled from hundreds to thousands – at least until the first deep snows of winter made the pastures impossible to reach. Meanwhile, in the district, reports were coming in of miracle cures, supposedly brought about when local invalids drank water procured from the stream on the mountain.

The various inquiries slowly rolled on as the years passed. Melanie and Maximin remained besieged in the convent but the nuns could do little to prevent waves of pilgrims virtually breaking into the place in order to catch a glimpse of, and if possible touch and talk to, the children.

It was five long years before Rome gave permission for Bishop de Bruillard to sanction the encounter on the mountain as a genuine vision and he was also authorized to start raising the money to build a church on the site. On 25 May 25 1851 the aging bishop himself, together with tens of thousands of others, climbed the mountain once again and laid the cornerstone of the new church.

Not that everyone was happy about the state of affairs. Some members of the various committees that had looked into the apparition remained skeptical about the whole business and one or two of them went to press to say so. Those upholding the validity of the apparition at La Salette suggest that these were all embittered people, who had their own agenda but it remains a fact that not everyone was convinced, either of the veracity of the vision itself, or regarding the honesty of Melanie and Maximin.

A later vision at Lourdes, of which we will hear more presently, eventually made a saint of the little girl who claimed to have seen the Virgin there. She is now St Bernadette of Lourdes. Bernadette entered a convent soon after the event and was happy to assume the role of a humble nun, which suited the Church down to the ground. Neither Melanie nor Maximin were quite so accommodating and sad to say the result of their encounter in September of 1846 led both of them to rather miserable lives and in both cases they died unfulfilled, frustrated, and virtually penniless.

Just prior to the laying of the cornerstone of the basilica on La Salette, Bishop de Bruillard had prevailed upon both children to divulge the nature of the individual secrets they had received from the Virgin. Maximin was fairly compliant but it took days of gentle pressure to convince Melanie that she should write down her secret. Even then she would do so only for the eyes of the Pope himself and for no other. The bishop persisted because he was anxious about what might happen if such sensitive information got into the wrong hands before the Vatican had seen it.

It was some time before the world became aware of either secret but they were both eventually published. Melanie had said all along that her secret was not to be divulged or published until the year 1858, on the strict instructions of the Virgin herself. Nobody knew for quite some time whether what lies below was the same as the secret Melanie vouchsafed to the Pope in 1851 but one Father Michael Corteville discovered the original documents buried away in the Vatican library in 1999.

Details of the original secrets were published by Fr Corteville in the year 2000 in a book entitled *La Grande Nouvelle des Bergers de la Salette*[1] The information in this work was dealt with again a couple of years later by Father René Laurentin, and the same Michel Corteville, in their book *Discovery of the Secret of La Salette*.[2] Photographs of the original documents, written by and signed by the two children, are reproduced in *Discovery of the Secret of La Salette*. We can be quite sure, therefore, that there was no substantial change between Melanie's secret as it was written down only a few years after the apparition at La Salette and the version published some years later.

I am including both secrets in full because although Melanie's at least is fairly lengthy, various parts of both messages will become more significant as our story unfolds.

MELANIE'S MESSAGE

1. "Melanie, what I am going to tell you now will not always be secret. You will be allowed to publish it in 1858."

2. "The priests, ministers of my Son, the priests, by their bad life, by their irreverences and their impiety in celebrating the holy mysteries, by love of money, love of honor and of pleasures, the priests have become cesspools of impurity. Yes, the priests are asking for vengeance, and vengeance is suspended over their heads. Woe to the priests and to persons consecrated to God, who by their infidelities and their bad life are crucifying anew my Son! The sins of persons consecrated to God cry out towards Heaven and call for vengeance, and see how vengeance is at their doors, because there is no longer found anyone to implore mercy and forgiveness for the people; there are no longer generous souls, there is no longer anyone worthy to offer the Victim without blemish to the Eternal on behalf of the world."

3. "God is going to strike in a manner without example."

---

1 Although this book is claimed to exist I can find no trace of its publication.
2 Rene Laurentin and Michel Corteville, Discovery of the Secret of La Salette, Fayard, Paris 2002.

4. "Woe to the inhabitants of the earth! God is going to exhaust His wrath, and no one will be able to take himself away from so many afflictions combined."

5. "The leaders, the guides of the people of God, have neglected prayer and penance, and the demon has obscured their intelligence; they have become these wandering stars that the old devil will drag along with his tail to make them perish. God will permit the old serpent to place divisions among rulers, in all societies and in all families; physical and moral pains will be suffered; God will abandon men to themselves, and will send chastisements which will follow one after another for more than thirty-five years."

6. "Society is on the eve of the most terrible scourges and of the greatest events; one must expect to be ruled with an iron rod and to drink the chalice of the wrath of God."

7. "May the Vicar of my Son, the sovereign Pontiff Pius IX, no longer leave Rome after the year 1859; but may he be firm and generous, may he fight with the weapons of faith and love; I will be with him."

8. "May he be wary of Napoleon; his heart is double, and when he will want to be at the same time Pope and emperor, soon God will withdraw from him: he is this eagle who, wanting always to raise himself up, will fall on the sword which he wanted to use in order to force the peoples to raise him up."

9. "Italy will be punished for her ambition in wanting to shake off the yoke of the Lord of Lords; also she will be delivered over to war; blood will flow on all sides; the churches will be closed or desecrated; the priests, the religious will be hunted; they will be made to die, and to die a cruel death. Several will abandon the faith, and the number of priests and religious who will separate themselves from the true religion will be great; among these persons there will be found even some bishops."

10. "May the Pope keep himself on guard against the performers of miracles, because the time has come when the most astonishing wonders will take place on the earth and in the air."

11. "In the year 1864, Lucifer with a great number of demons will be unleashed from hell; they will abolish the faith little by little and even in persons consecrated

to God; they will blind them in such a way that barring a particular grace these persons will take on the spirit of these bad angels: several religious houses will lose the faith entirely and will lose many souls."

12. "Bad books will abound on earth, and the spirits of darkness will spread everywhere a universal slackening in all that concerns the service of God; they will have a very great power over nature: there will be churches to serve these spirits. Some persons will be transported from one place to another by these bad spirits and even some priests, because they will not be guiding themselves by the good spirit of the Gospel, which is a spirit of humility, charity and zeal for the glory of God. The dead and the just will be made to revive." [That is to say that these dead will take the appearance of just souls who had lived on earth, so as to better mislead men: these so-called resurrected dead, who will be nothing other than the demon under these appearances, will preach another Gospel contrary to the one of the true Christ Jesus, denying the existence of heaven, or they may also be the souls of the damned. All these souls will appear as if united to their bodies.] "There will be in all places extraordinary wonders, because the true faith is dying out and because false light enlightens the world. Woe to the Princes of the Church who will not be occupied except to pile riches upon riches, to safeguard their authority and to dominate with pride."

13. "The Vicar of my Son will have much to suffer, because for a time the Church will be delivered over to great persecutions: this will be the time of darkness; the Church will have a frightful crisis."

14. "The holy faith of God being forgotten, each individual will want to be guided by himself and to be superior to his peers. Civil and ecclesiastical powers will be abolished, all order and all justice will be trampled underfoot; one will see only homicides, hatred, jealousy, lying, and discord, without love for country, or for family."

15. "The Holy Father will suffer much. I will be with him until the end to receive his sacrifice."

16. "The wicked will make an attempt several times on his life without power to do harm to his days; but neither he, nor his successor [who will not reign long,] will see the triumph of the Church of God."

17. "Civil rulers will have all one same design which will be to abolish, and to make disappear, all religious principle, in order to make way for materialism, atheism, spiritualism, and all kinds of vices."

18. "In the year 1865, the abomination will be seen in holy places; in convents, the flowers of the Church will be decayed and the demon will make himself as the king of hearts. May those who are at the head of religious communities keep themselves on guard for persons whom they must receive, because the demon will use all of his malice in order to introduce into religious Orders persons devoted to sin, for disorders and the love of carnal pleasures will be spread by all the earth."

19. "France, Italy, Spain, and England will be in war; blood will flow in the streets; Frenchman will fight with Frenchman, Italian with Italian; subsequently there will be a general war which will be appalling. For a time, God will no longer be mindful of France or Italy, because the Gospel of Jesus Christ is no longer known. The wicked will deploy all their malice; they will kill themselves, they will massacre themselves mutually even in the houses."

20. "At the first stroke of His lightning sword, the mountains and the whole of nature will tremble with terror, because the disorders and the crimes of men pierce the vault of the heavens. Paris will be burned and Marseilles engulfed; several great cities will be shaken and engulfed by earthquakes; it will be believed that all is lost; only homicides will be seen, only the noise of weapons and blasphemies will be heard. The just will suffer much; their prayers, their penances, and their tears will climb even up to heaven and all the people of God will ask for forgiveness and mercy, and will ask for my help and my intercession. Then Jesus Christ by an act of His justice and of His great mercy for the just, will command to His angels that all His enemies be put to death. All at once the persecutors of the Church of Jesus Christ and all men devoted to sin will perish, and the earth will become like a desert. Then peace, the reconciliation of God with men will be made; Jesus Christ will be served, adored, and glorified; charity will flower everywhere. The new kings will be the right arm of the holy Church, which will be strong, humble, pious, poor, zealous, and imitator of the virtues of Jesus Christ. The Gospel will be preached everywhere and men will make great progress in the faith, because there will be unity among the workers of Jesus Christ and because men will live in the fear of God."

21. "This peace among men will not be long; 25 years of abundant harvests will make them forget that the sins of men are the cause of all the pains which come upon the earth."

22. "A forerunner of the antichrist with his troops from several nations will fight against the true Christ, the only Savior of the world; he will spill much blood, and will want to annihilate the worship of God in order to make himself be looked upon as a God."

23. "The earth will be struck all kinds of plagues [in addition to pestilence and famine which will be general]; there will be wars until the last war, which will then be made by the ten kings of the antichrist, which kings will have all one same design and will be the only ones who will rule the world. Before these arrive, there will be a type of false peace in the world; one will think only about amusing oneself; the wicked will deliver themselves over to all kinds of sin, but the children of the holy Church, the children of the faith, my true imitators, will grow in the love of God and in the virtues which are dear to me. Happy the humble souls guided by the Holy Spirit! I will fight with them until they arrive at the fullness of the age."

24. "Nature is asking for vengeance for men, and she shudders with terror in waiting for that which must come upon the earth soiled with crimes."

25. "Tremble, earth, and you who make profession of serving Jesus Christ and who on the inside adore yourselves, tremble; for God is going to deliver you over to His enemy, because the holy places are in corruption; many convents are no longer houses of God, but the pastures of Asmodeas and his sort."

26. "It will be during this time that the antichrist will be born of a Hebrew religious, of a false Virgin who will have communication with the old serpent, the master of impurity; his father will be Bishop; at birth, he will vomit blasphemies, he will have teeth; in a word, this will be the devil incarnate; he will let out frightening cries, he will perform wonders, he will nourish himself only on impurities. He will have brothers who, although they will not be like him demons incarnate, will be children of evil; at twelve years, they will make themselves noticed by their brilliant victories which they will win; soon, they will each be at the head of armies, assisted by the legions of hell."

27. "The seasons will be changed, the earth will produce only bad fruits, the stars will lose their regular movements, the moon will reflect only a feeble reddish light; water and fire will give to the globe of the earth convulsive movements and horrible earthquakes which will cause to be engulfed mountains, cities [etc.]."

28. "Rome will lose the faith and become the seat of the antichrist."

29. "The demons of the air with the antichrist will perform great wonders on the earth and in the air, and men will corrupt themselves more and more. God will have care of His faithful servants and men of goodwill; the Gospel will be preached everywhere, all peoples and all nations will have knowledge of the truth!"

30. "I address a pressing appeal to the earth: I call upon the true disciples of God living and reigning in the heavens; I call upon the true imitators of Christ made man, the only and true Savior of men; I call upon my children, my true devotees, those who have given themselves to me so that I may guide them to my divine Son, those whom I carry so to speak in my arms, those who have lived by my spirit; finally I call upon the Apostles of the last times, the faithful disciples of Jesus Christ who have lived in contempt for the world and for themselves, in poverty and in humility, in contempt and in silence, in prayer and in mortification, in chastity and in union with God, in suffering and unknown to the world. It is time that they go out and come to enlighten the earth. Go, and show yourselves as my dear children; I am with you and in you, provided that your faith is the light which enlightens you in these days of woe. May your zeal render you like the starving for the glory and honor of Jesus Christ. Fight, children of light, you the small number who can see; for behold the time of times, the end of ends."

31. "The Church will be eclipsed, the world will be in consternation. But behold Enoch and Elie filled with the Spirit of God; they will preach with the strength of God, and men of goodwill will believe in God, and many souls will be consoled; they will make great progress by the virtue of the Holy Spirit and will condemn the devilish errors of the antichrist."

32. "Woe to the inhabitants of the earth! There will be bloody wars and famines; pestilences and contagious diseases; there will be rains of a dreadful hail of animals, thunders which will shake cities, earthquakes which will engulf countries; voices will be heard in the air, men will beat their head against the walls, they will call upon

death, and on another side death will be their torture; blood will flow on all sides. Who will be able to overcome, if God does not shorten the time of the ordeal? By the blood, the tears, and the prayers of the just, God will let Himself be swayed, Enoch and Elie will be put to death; pagan Rome will disappear; fire from Heaven will fall and will consume three cities; all the universe will be struck with terror, and many will let themselves be misled because they have not adored the true Christ living among them. It is time; the sun darkens; faith alone will live."

33. "Behold the time; the abyss opens. Behold the king of kings of darkness. Behold the beast with his subjects, calling himself the savior of the world. He will raise himself up with pride into the air in order to go even up to heaven; he will be smothered by the breath of the holy Archangel Michael. He will fall, and the earth, which for three days will be in continual evolutions, will open its bosom full of fire; he will be plunged forever with all his own into the eternal chasms of hell. Then water and fire will purify the earth and will consume all the works of the pride of men, and all will be renewed: God will be served and glorified."

MAXIMIN'S MESSAGE

"If my people continue, what I will say to you will arrive earlier, if it changes a little, it will be a little later.

"France has corrupted the universe, one day it will be punished. The faith will die out in France: three quarters of France will not practice religion anymore, or almost no more, the other part will practice it without really practicing it. Then, after [that], nations will convert, the faith will be rekindled everywhere. A great country, now Protestant, in the north of Europe, will be converted; by the support of this country all the other nations of the world will be converted.

"Before all that arrives, great disorders will arrive, in the Church, and everywhere. Then, after [that], our Holy Father the Pope will be persecuted. His successor will be a pontiff that nobody expects.

"Then, after [that], a great peace will come, but it will not last a long time. A monster will come to disturb it.

"All that I tell you here will arrive in the other century, at the latest in the year two thousand."

La Salette eventually came to support its own Order of nuns and now has a fine church with priests to attend to the needs of those who still travel there. In the years that followed, poor Maximin wandered round from one seminar to another, and after a short spell with the Vatican Guard in Italy, he took to the life of a virtual vagrant. Always cheerful and optimistic about his own ability to make a mark on life the fact is that Maximin was incapable of either discipline or concentration. He died at the age of 40, back in Corps, in the same house he had lived in as a child. He was penniless and had known long periods of hunger, even as an adult.

Melanie certainly lived longer, but fared no better than Maximin. On at least three separate occasions she joined religious Orders, only to be dismissed in each case because she could not settle to the necessary discipline of the veil. As an adult she claimed to have been subject to visions since early childhood but there was absolutely no evidence of this at the time of the La Salette vision. She regularly disagreed with high-ranking leaders of the Catholic Church and was even threatened with excommunication on at least one occasion. She died at the age of 71 in Italy, an embittered elderly woman. Melanie Calvet ended her days as an exile from her own land and in her later years at least she was considered by many to be at best eccentric and at worst some sort of fraudster.

Pilgrims still travel to that remote part of South West France but the Church itself is certainly less keen to champion the vision at La Salette than the more famous one that took place at Lourdes, also in France. The very nature of the words spoken by the Virgin Mary at La Salette is probably the main reason, and in particular the start of the secret vouchsafed to Melanie Calvet:

> The priests, ministers of my Son, the priests, by their bad life, by their irreverences and their impiety in celebrating the holy mysteries, by love of money, love of honor and of pleasures, the priests have become cesspools of impurity. Yes, the priests are asking for vengeance, and vengeance is suspended over their heads. Woe to the priests and to persons consecrated to God, who by their infidelities and their bad life are crucifying anew my Son!

As far as I can ascertain Roman Catholics are still prohibited, by a direct order from the Vatican, from openly discussing the "nature" of the La Salette vision or from publishing anything about it. At least part of the reason for this is because persistent rumors started to circulate later in the nineteenth century that the vision on La Salette had been stage-managed and that the unsuspecting children had been duped on that beautiful September day. What makes matters worse as far as the Church is concerned is that it has been continually suggested that the hoax was perpetrated by Freemasons!

Chapter Three

Stranger and Stranger

STRANGER AND STRANGER

I first read of the La Salette vision of the Virgin Mary about fifteen years ago. At the time the account meant very little to me. Although I found the story fascinating it did not relate to my research at that time. It wasn't until some two years later that the La Salette vision came back to me and when it did so, it became significant for a whole host of reasons.

La Salette returned to my mind, not so much because of what supposedly happened there, but because of "where" the village was in a geographic sense. During the last two decades I have undertaken a great deal of research into ancient geometry. This had come about as a result of the work of a Scot called Professor Alexander Thom. He had spent fifty painstaking years carefully measuring the ancient standing stones, circles, and avenues that are to be found from Scotland in the North, right down to Brittany in the South. Some of these monuments are as much as 5,000 years old and Professor Thom had a hunch that they might have been erected as a means of tracking the stars and planets, and in particular the moon.

Professor Thom discovered that our ancient Megalithic ancestors had used a specific unit of linear length when they had so carefully constructed the circles and alignments. He called it the Megalithic Yard. No matter where he found it, the Megalithic Yard never varied by more than 1 part in 500 and it was 82.966cm in length. At first on my own, and then in the company of a colleague, Christopher Knight, I began to look at the Megalithic Yard very carefully. What we eventually discovered was that underpinning the efforts of the Megalithic builders lay a deep understanding, not only of geometry, but of the very size and shape of the earth. Details of this research can be found in *The Bronze Age Computer Disc*[1] and in *Civilization One.*[2]

Soon after writing *The Bronze Age Computer Disc*, I chanced upon the work of a French researcher, whose name was Xavier Guichard. Guichard was a high-ranking Parisian police officer but in his spare time he was a historian, with a penchant for maps and geography. Guichard had discovered something both surprising and, at first sight, very unlikely. He had noticed that certain place names in France that had an "al" component, for example, Alaise and Falaise, when joined

---

1 Alan Butler, The Bronze Age Computer Disc, Quantum, London, 1999.
2 Christopher Knight and Alan Butler, Civilization One, Watkins Publishing, London, 2004.

together on maps, produced dead straight lines that ran either North/South or East/West. He couldn't really explain these discoveries but thought that he had happened upon a series of very carefully created paths, first used in the Bronze Age. These, he conjectured, might have been tracks specifically created to facilitate the movement of salt from one place to another.

The association with salt came about because Guichard concluded that the "Al" part of the place names concerned was from an ancient work "Hal" which means salt.

Guichard noticed that the North/South and East/West lines were almost 1° of the earth's surface apart, but not exactly. In reality they were about 1' of arc closer together and he reasoned that this was the case because those creating the lines did not have an absolute knowledge of the true circumference of the earth. Meanwhile, the form of ancient geometry I had rediscovered, and proved with Christopher Knight, had been slightly different than the one we use today. Instead of circles containing 360°, the Megalithic model had relied on 366° circles. When this form of geometry was applied to Guichard's strange lines, they proved to be unerringly accurate and were precisely 1° apart in Megalithic terms.

Xavier Guichard had suggested that the prime meridian of this whole system lay at what we would now call 6° East of Greenwich, and he identified a little town called Alaise, in Southeast France, as being the most important location of all. (The prime meridian used by the world these days is a line that runs from the North Pole, through Greenwich near London, England, and onto the South Pole. This line as classified as being at 0° longitude.)

It eventually occurred to me that the little village of La Salette, and in particular the mountain where the vision had taken place, was in a direct line with Alaise. Like Alaise, La Salette stands at a longitude 6° East of Greenwich. What is more, I couldn't help but notice that the name of the place, which almost certainly means "little salt" had a connection with Guichard's insistence that villages and towns on the lines had names that somehow reflected an association with salt.

Being on what Guichard had assessed to be the most significant longitudinal line from prehistory, it seemed that La Salette might be worthy of more attention. From childhood I have been fascinated by astronomy and its ancient cousin astrology. I have studied both intently and, together with the apparent significance of the place, this had led to a hunch regarding the La Salette vision and the suggestion that the whole business had been a hoax, perpetrated for some reason by Freemasons. In order to reassure myself that I was most probably wrong, I created an astrological chart, not only for the day on which the La Salette vision took place, but also for the time of the apparition. When I looked at this chart my eyes nearly popped out of their sockets.

An astrological chart is nothing more or less than a map of the sky at any specific point in time. The most common form of astrology known to the world these days is personal or natal astrology. The theory is that if an astrological chart is drawn up for the time, place, and date of a person's birth, the position of the sun, moon, and planets and the angular relationships they have one with another, gives an indication of the character and capabilities of the person in question. However, this isn't how astrology started. There was a time at which astrology and astronomy were indistinguishable. (Astronomy is a study of the stars and planets from a purely scientific viewpoint.) All early cultures were fascinated by the sky. They saw the sun, moon, and planets as deities and believed that their position at any given time had a big part to play in the way events on earth were likely to unfold.

As seen from the earth the sun, moon, and all the planets circle within a belt around the earth that runs slightly North and South of the equator. This is known as the "plane of the ecliptic." As shown below, the stars occupying this belt of heaven have been historically divided into twelve segments. These are known as the signs of the zodiac. The sun, moon, and planets appear to travel within this backdrop of stars and by way of the zodiac it is possible to map where they are at any given point in time.

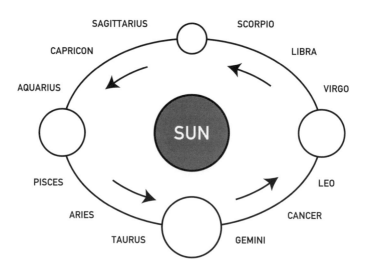

The path the earth and all the other planets take around the sun is known as the plane of the ecliptic. Because of our position in the solar system it appears that the sun is also moving. So it seems to us that the sun, moon, and the rest of the planets move within this particular band of the heavens. Historically we have split this band into twelve segments, distinguished by groups or constellations of stars. This is the zodiac.

Whether or not readers of this book have the remotest confidence in the ability of the stars and planets to affect or reflect in any way our destiny or character is not really of any importance in terms of the La Salette vision. What matters is that certain planetary positions have, since very ancient times, been associated with very specific happenings here on earth. In other words, as we shall see, the astrological chart for the La Salette vision might mean little or nothing to us, but it would certainly have meant a great deal to someone. Almost any research astrologer would immediately recognize the significance of the positions of the sun, moon, and planets on that day, in relation to the vision itself.

But even before we look closely at the La Salette astrological chart we need to bear in mind exactly "when" the event occurred. It took place on 19 September 1846. This date is as important in a religious sense as in an astronomical or astrological one. The day of the vision was a Saturday. In Catholic terms this day was the eve of the feast of "Our Lady of Sorrows." The feast of Our Lady of Sorrows dates back to at least the start of the fifteenth century, at which time it was celebrated on the Friday after the third Sunday after Easter. It commemorates the sorrows of the Virgin Mary with regard to her son Jesus. Specifically, the seven sorrows are: The prophecy of Simeon; the flight into Egypt; the loss of the Child Jesus in the temple; the meeting of Jesus and Mary on the Way of the Cross; the Crucifixion; the taking down of the body of Jesus from the Cross; and the burial of Jesus.

For some centuries a feast of Our Lady of Sorrows has been held on the third Sunday of September. There is a specific Mass or religious service dedicated to the Seven Sorrows of Our Lady that is celebrated at this time. (A 'feast' in this sense has nothing to do with a meal of any sort.)

Since the vision took place on the eve of the feast of Our Lady of Sorrows, it would have seemed entirely appropriate to those monitoring the story of Melanie and Maximin at La Salette that the Virgin Mary, as they saw her on 19 September, was weeping. However, the children themselves were ignorant of such matters so it is unlikely that they made any such connection.

Why the feast of Our Lady of Sorrows found its way to this date in the religious calendar is illuminating in itself. September, in the Northern hemisphere at least, is around the beginning of autumn, and is a period of harvest and abundance. Historically, wheat and other grain products were being cut at this time and fruits were appearing on trees and bushes. It is in late August and through much of September that the sun occupies the zodiac sign of Virgo, which literally means "Virgin." The symbol for this zodiac sign is a beautiful young woman and has been since the most ancient times. It is easy to see why this should be the case. The very earliest religions of the world were "feminine" oriented, with religious adherents giving special reverence to "the Great Mother Goddess." The fertility of this goddess was said to be responsible for all that humanity needed in order to survive.

It was believed that all the food that sustained us came directly from the Great Goddess, who literally represented the earth itself. It is not surprising, therefore, that many of the major celebrations from ancient history that extolled the power and compassion of the Great Goddess took place at this time of year, when food was available in plenty and veneration and thanks were most appropriate.

The message of the Virgin Mary at La Salette was specifically related to the harvest, with dire warnings that both the wheat crop and that of the potatoes and vines would fail if people did not look more closely at their religious lives and observances. In other words, there is already something very ancient and pagan about the circumstances of the message the two children received.

Because of the day on which the vision took place, 19 September, it was inevitable that the sun would be in the zodiac sign of Virgo, but what surprised me when I looked at the astrological chart for the day in question was that it was far from being alone there. Joining the sun in Virgo was the moon, Mercury, Venus, and also the planet Mars. This is an unusual state of affairs and might only be expected to happen very rarely on any given day in a particular year, in this case a day that was the eve of Our Lady of Sorrows.

The planet Venus would have represented a beautiful sight on that clear morning as the children had left Ablandins. It occupied a zodiac position of 4° of Virgo, whereas the sun was at 26° of Virgo. This means that at this time Venus was a morning star and rose into the sky '88 minutes' ahead of the sun. At the time Venus was just about as bright as it can be when viewed from the earth. Next to the sun and the moon the planet Venus is the brightest object in our skies. Even more significant is the fact that the event took place the day before the new moon. On the day of the vision the moon was nothing more than a tiny crescent, rising half an hour after Venus. It must have looked glorious, sparkling in the reflected light of the approaching dawn, but it certainly wasn't bright. For quite some time Venus would have been the single most significant object in the Eastern sky and we shall see presently that Venus as a bright morning star has its own very important connotations. But could there have been any special significance to the prominent position of Venus on that day? Indeed there could. If Virgo is the zodiac sign dedicated to the Great Goddess in her manifestation as the Virgin, Venus is her planet. Practically every culture in the world has dedicated Venus to the Goddess and of course even in our language the name of the planet is borrowed from Latin and represented the goddess of Love and Fertility.

There is much more to say about these matters but when one bears in mind the events that took place that day, the chances of the planets being in this position at such an auspicious time by accident is so remote as to be virtually ridiculous. This leads to one of two inevitable conclusions;

1. The vision was genuine and the arrangement of the planets on that day was part of the "miracle" of La Salette, or
2. Whoever "stage-managed" the events at La Salette had deliberately chosen the most significant astronomical and religious moment to do so.

Over the centuries there have been many sightings of the Virgin Mary reported, and in many different parts of the globe. The most famous are the Lourdes apparition, which took place in Lourdes, France in 1858 and the vision at Fatima, Portugal in 1917. In neither of these examples, or any of the others from history at which I have looked closely, were the skies so neatly arranged or the religious calendar so well ordered as was the case in the vision of La Salette. This immediately sets the La Salette happening apart as something very special and certainly worthy of more attention.

Although the Catholic Church, after careful consideration, was willing to put out an edict that the La Salette occurrence had been a genuine visitation of the Virgin Mary, it lived to regret having done so. In reality it probably did not have much choice. By the time the examination of all the relevant details was completed, there were already tens of thousands of pilgrims making their way up the mountain every year. The Pope was already in possession of the "secrets" said to have been vouchsafed to the children by the Virgin and these must have worried him, particularly that of Melanie. From the very start Melanie's secret was scathing with regard to certain ministers of the Church, a state of affairs that must also have alarmed many in the corridors of the Vatican. However, for the Church to ignore La Salette, or worse still to condemn it, would have been to create a "schism" that might have proved very damaging in itself. Thus we find the Pope faced with a virtual fait accompli and a damage-limiting exercise commenced almost immediately. This has not been handled well over the years.

Although the Church still upholds the genuine nature of the La Salette vision, it has taken the peculiar step of forbidding Catholics to discuss or write about it in detail. In other words, the position of the Church seems to be that Catholics can "accept" the visitation of the Virgin at La Salette; they can go there to worship and to ask for the intercession of the Blessed Virgin, but they cannot go to press about what happened there (at least not without the express permission of the Vatican). This is something of a mystery and is certainly not the case with regard to the even more famous vision of the Virgin Mary at Lourdes. It isn't hard to see why. The Virgin Mary who appeared at Lourdes was much less political and seems to have conformed in every way to what the Catholic Church expected of her, even very conveniently referring to herself as "the immaculate conception." (Convenient bearing in mind that the immaculate conception was being hotly debated by the Church at the time of the Lourdes vision and had been made canon law in 1854.)

It was, and is, the overtly political nature of the La Salette vision that upsets the Vatican and this is also why so much attention is given these days to Lourdes, with the much more impressive and, at the time, popular La Salette vision now being marginalized. But there is almost certainly another reason why La Salette is such a potential embarrassment and that is the persistent rumor that the vision was a fraud, deliberately perpetrated to achieve the ends that ultimately came about: to embarrass and confound the Vatican and to sew dissent amongst believers. What makes matters worse is that the most likely culprit for the staging of the La Salette vision is Freemasonry.

This assertion is never, ever mentioned by the Church itself and could be one of the main reasons why it specifically forbids discussion of the La Salette vision. Perhaps fortunately for those of us who prefer to reach the truth by our own means the Catholic Church has no control over those who lie beyond its own jurisdiction and so the rumors persist.

There was a specific reason for my surprise regarding the astrological chart I had drawn up for the incident of La Salette, apart from its unlikely configurations. The fact was that I had seen very similar charts before, and they had always been in connection with Freemasonry. Perhaps the rumor wasn't so far-fetched after all.

There is probably no organization in the world that is more hated, loathed, and castigated by the Catholic Church than Freemasonry. Much of the rest of this book is dedicated to explaining why this should be the case. However, in order to fully understand these matters it is first necessary to take a closer look at Freemasonry, its origins, beliefs, and practices.

CHAPTER FOUR

INSIDE THE LODGE

INSIDE THE LODGE

There is no single definition of what Freemasonry actually is but its own members generally describe it as: "a system of morality, veiled in allegory and illustrated by symbols."

If anyone were to visit the average Masonic Lodge in the Western world today they would find there a group of men (though there are women's lodges these days). They could observe that these men participated in what would appear to be quite strange observances and practices. These involve special clothing, a host of symbols within the surroundings, specific gestures and movements, and the reciting of long passages of more or less incomprehensible verses. Outside of the ceremony the observer might be forgiven for believing that the average Masonic Lodge is little more than a social club, where money is collected for good causes and where a great deal of eating and drinking takes place.

As with practically everything in Freemasonry, its origins are shrouded in mystery. In a modern sense Freemasonry came into being in the year 1717 in London, England when a group of four existent Lodges joined together to create "Grand Lodge," which still exists and which regulates Freemasonry throughout England. However, this is certainly not the starting point of what its members know as "the Craft." As its name implies much in Freemasonry is based upon the ancient profession of stonemasonry, which was of great importance in Europe from medieval times onwards. Because of the significance of the art of stonemasonry, which was necessary in particular for the creation of great castles and stupendous churches across the continent, stonemasons soon became organized into self-help groups known as guilds.

Guilds existed for most crafts and professions during the Middle Ages but that of the masons was, arguably, the oldest of them all. A guild was a cross between a trade union and a trade federation because its aims and objectives served everyone in that particular occupation, from the lowest to the highest. Guilds were fiercely independent and would not allow freebooters to impinge on their monopolies in any specific region, town, or city. As often as not a particular trade passed from father to son. In the case of stonemasons this might mean that several generations of any particular family would work on the same project, especially if it was something as huge as one of the great Gothic cathedrals that were springing up everywhere during the Middle Ages and which took centuries to complete.

Modern Freemasons are most certainly associated with the origins of the guild system in stonemasonry but there are significant differences. Freemasons refer to themselves as being "speculative" in the sense that none or at least very few of them have anything to do with cutting, dressing, or erecting stone. It is simply that the origin of the practices and ordinances of Freemasonry relate to the terminology and sometimes the history of the stonemasons' guilds.

In terms of its ritual, Freemasonry concerns itself with the creation of a very specific building from history – the Temple of Solomon that was built in Jerusalem around 3,000 years ago. It might seem particularly odd that such an ancient building project could have anything at all to do with what amounts to a mutual-aid and social club in the twenty-first century. However, the very kernel of Freemasonic practice is so deeply entwined with the myth and mystery of Solomon's Temple that this great building, at least in a symbolic sense, "is" the essence of Freemasonry.

There are plenty of Freemasons, and others, who lay claim to the Craft being far older than the eighteenth century, when it was first formalized in Britain. The oldest known Masonic document goes back to 1390 but in terms of the subject matter of Masonic legends this might as well be yesterday. Most of the ritual used in Freemasonry is couched in language that is eighteenth-century or earlier in origin but what proves to be most fascinating about the Craft is not what is obvious to the observer but rather what lies below the surface.

Every aspirant joining Freemasonry must undergo three stages or "degrees" of initiation before he becomes what is known as a "Master Mason." These are essentially ceremonies, undertaken by the members of the Lodge as a whole. At each stage the aspirant embarks on a series of ritual journeys. Through allegorical stories, many relating to Solomon's Temple, and specific oaths, he gradually rises up the three degrees of Freemasonry to join his brethren on the essential platform of the Craft – the position of Master Mason. Beyond this point there are various positions within the Lodge that a Mason can take on, for example Junior Warden or Worshipful Master. Indeed, some forms of Freemasonry have other ceremonies and practices that can take the willing brother through a whole series of "degrees" right up to 33rd degree Mason, or even further in some cases.

What really annoys many people regarding Freemasonry is its apparent secrecy, together with the fact that it has been, for centuries, a very insular society. In other words, Masons willingly undertake to assist other Masons, ostensibly before they will help anyone else. Despite the fact that many modern Freemasons say this is an archaic tradition, the commitment to behave in this way is still enshrined in the oaths Freemasons take. I for one can see nothing at all strange in this. Anyone who has ever been in a trade union, a particular religious denomination, or even the Boy Scouts makes more or less the same sort of commitment, either in words or by implication.

The slightly less savory side to this, however, is that Freemasons have been accused for decades of helping each other to such an extent that their actions could be seen as being at best dubious and at worst downright illegal. For example, it has been suggested that Masonic judges have been lenient with those of a Masonic bent who appear before them in court. Similarly, in large business undertakings it is asserted that Freemasons have formed what amounts to cartels, in order to give contract work to their own brethren. Human nature being what it is there is little doubt that such things have gone on and while these situations are not to be condoned, they can hardly be said to be exclusive to Freemasonry.

Freemasonry is replete with what looks to the rest of the world like strange symbols, some of which have brought upon the Craft the accusation of Satanism. I have looked carefully at the Craft for a couple of decades now and since I am not a Freemason myself I have no particular axe to grind. I personally have found nothing to indicate that there is anything within the Craft, apart from misunderstood symbolism and ritual, that could be termed Satanic. Indeed, the ideals of Freemasons are as laudable in a social and moral sense as those of almost any religious group. This might be part of the problem because Freemasonry claims, often too vehemently for its own good, that it is not a religion. Despite this assertion, it is not possible to be both a Freemason and, for example, an atheist (except in France). Every would-be Mason has to profess a belief in God, though there is nothing in the ritual to suggest what this "God" actually represents to any given individual. The general terms for God within Freemasonry are "The Great Geometrician" or "Great Architect of the Universe" and the definition of this power is left perhaps deliberately ambiguous so that "men of good conscience'" of any religious persuasion can become Freemasons.

In fairly recent times interest in Freemasonry has increased significantly, and so has criticism of its aims, objectives, and its very existence. Freemasonry has always been hated by many orthodox Christian believers, though why this should be the case is far from clear and appears to come about for a host of more or less understood reasons. It is obvious that this hatred and mistrust emanates from the leaders of Church denominations, for example the Pope in the case of Catholics. Perhaps this isn't too surprising. History and experience show that, generally speaking, no "power base" has much truck with another power base that might subvert its own influence and authority.

Strangely enough, Freemasonry itself is different with this regard. It doesn't care what its members believe, just as long as the existence of a supreme deity is accepted. Freemasons can be Christians, Hindus, Jews, Muslims, or from any other religion, orthodox or otherwise. What is more, oaths taken by aspiring Masons make it plain that their allegiance to country and to family should come before their commitment to the Craft. The espoused objectives of Freemasonry are essentially moral rather than religious and maybe, together with the inherent secrecy of the Craft, this is also part of the problem. However, it has been clear to me for some time that in the case of the Catholic Church there are deeper and more serious issues at stake.

As far as secrecy is concerned, it is true that Freemasons take the most horrific oaths not to reveal specific words, handshakes, and gestures from their rituals. They acknowledge that if they do spill the beans they can be hanged, disemboweled, and left to the mercy of the rising tide. These are historic and symbolic words and there surely isn't a Freemason in the world these days who sees this as anything more than an interesting historical legacy, born in a period when secrets really had to be kept for the good of all. In fact there is very little, if anything, within Freemasonry that cannot now be discovered in the reference section of any public library or on the Internet. Far more is now known about the internal workings and rituals of the Craft than that of many of the sects and organizations that seek to attack and ultimately destroy it. What is more, when one does learn the deepest secrets of Freemasonry they appear, to the layperson, to be nonsense.

No amount of reasoned argument will prevent some authorities and individuals from castigating Freemasonry, or from being convinced that the whole Craft is a tool of the Devil, intent on bringing down all religious belief and ultimately destroying society. It is accepted by some historians that the seeds of this animosity were probably set in the eighteenth and nineteenth centuries, when the orthodox Church was losing power, while the liberality of advancing society saw a similarity of purpose with Freemasonic ideals. As we shall see, many of those who advocated revolution in both France and America were Freemasons. Meanwhile, the forces that sought to quell civil unrest and to maintain the status quo during this period were responsive to the Catholic Church and the old Protestant denominations of Britain and the Continent. To some of the diehard establishment figures, especially those with an aristocratic or royal background, Freemasonry was synonymous with anarchy and the destruction of all they saw as civilized values. If the Craft also attacked the Church, it was therefore clearly the work of Satan.

There are a number of different varieties of Freemasonry in existence in the world today but by far the majority of Freemasons can be split into two groups, known as the "ancients" and the "moderns." At the time Freemasonry first appeared in England, it had a strong Catholic bias because it evolved first in Scotland, well before the Reformation that saw the Protestants coming to power. Many Scottish lodges predate those in England or at the very least there are no reliable records for early English Freemasonry. When Freemasonry is known to have come South of the border, during the reign of King James I of England and VI of Scotland (1566–1625), it retained many of its Catholic brothers. James himself was nominally Protestant but there were always accusations, both regarding James, his son, and his grandsons, that they were closet Catholics.

The progress of Freemasonry from this point is intricately tied to what was happening within Britain. The son of James I, King Charles I, who reigned from 1625 to 1649, was also nominally Protestant, but he had a Catholic wife and it was always suggested that his personal leanings were toward Rome. Whatever his true religious persuasion, Charles was very autocratic and believed in the divine right of kings. In other words, he held to the conviction that in his decisions and actions he was responsive to no human authority but only that of God. England had been Protestant since King Henry VIII (1491–1547) had broken with Rome and established the English Church, with himself as its head. However, a newer and far more pure form of Protestantism had gradually found its way to England. Many of the merchants and squires were, by the reign of Charles I, known as Puritans.

The Puritans did not accept Charles' belief in the divine right of kings, What is more, they remained adamant that any king should rule with the sanction of his subjects, in the form of a parliament. The stage was set for a bitter civil war in England. This lasted from 1642 until 1648 and resulted in the forces of the king being soundly beaten by those of Parliament. When Charles would not agree to the terms put to him, he was tried for treason and executed in London in 1649.

There followed a period of eleven years that is generally referred to as "The Commonwealth." Although England was nominally ruled by Parliament at this time, in the main it was responsive to one man. He was a leading Parliamentarian general called Oliver Cromwell. Cromwell became Lord Protector, which was as good as being a king. Freemasonry in England most certainly found itself in a difficult position during the Commonwealth because it had shown a strong bias for the Stuart kings and retained its old Catholic affiliations. As a result we don't hear anything about English Freemasonry during these eleven years because the people concerned were clearly keeping their heads down.

When Oliver Cromwell died in 1658, England fell into a state of turmoil. This resulted in the son of Charles I, another Charles, being invited to return from exile in France to become King Charles II of England. He began his reign in 1660 and this is precisely the time that we see Freemasonry in England beginning to gain ground. People who had been closet Freemasons now began to rise to power within government and especially in science, but there were to be further setbacks.

When Charles II died in 1685, he was without an heir. This meant that the throne went to his brother, James, who was duly crowned King James II. While James I, Charles I, and Charles II had all respected the Protestant religion as being that of England, James II was different. He was a devout Catholic and it became clear that he intended to steer England back toward Rome. This was not acceptable to the majority of Parliamentarians and James was deposed in 1688. His daughter, Mary, was invited to take the throne, together with her Protestant Dutch husband, William of Orange. After them came Queen Anne, another daughter of James. When Anne died without issue in 1714, the English authorities cast around for a suitable candidate and eventually settled on George, Elector of Hanover. His rightful claim to the English throne was tenuous but he was a staunch Protestant and that was what really mattered.

During the years that England had struggled under successive Stuart monarchs, Freemasonry had gone through some difficult times. Under the reigns of William and Mary, and Queen Anne, and especially at the accession of George I, the Stuart kings in exile in France continued to fight for the English throne. Scottish Freemasons became associated with this struggle and were often accused of being Jacobites, the name given to the Stuart supporters. Finally, with the crowning of George I, English Freemasonry had to rebuild itself if it wished to survive. It needed a more respectable face and one that would sit easily with the new dynasty.

Grand Lodge was formed in 1717, when four existing London Lodges came together. The need for political expediency caused a schism within Freemasonry between those who wished to fall in line with the needs of the moment and those who wanted to see Freemasonry retain its old roots. Thus the "ancients" and "moderns" came into existence. Ultimately the breach was healed but many other branches of Freemasonry gradually developed and still exist around the world. Some of them, York Rite Freemasonry for example, have differences in terms of their historical perspective, while organizations such as the "Shriners" are peculiarly American in origin, though are still Masonic in nature. Scottish Rite Freemasonry has its origins in France around 1737 and Grand Orient French Freemasonry probably dates from around the same period.

Apart from the more "exotic" forms of Freemasonry, most branches of the Craft are agreed on the three stages of becoming a fully-fledged Freemason. The first step is to become an "Entered Apprentice." During the ceremony the candidate wears a hood and must bare his chest. He receives instructions as to the history and significance of Freemasonry. It is at this time he is first introduced to King Solomon's Temple.

The second degree is that of "Fellowcraft." The candidate has to prove that he has learned the lessons of the first degree and that he is fit to proceed further into the Craft. He is introduced to further information about King Solomon's Temple and its importance to Freemasonry.

Finally comes the third-degree ceremony, after which the candidate will become a "Master Mason." This is the most symbolic of the three degrees and during the proceedings the candidate ritually dies and is reborn into the rights and privileges of Freemasonry. At this time the candidate "becomes" the fallen Hiram Abif, who was supposedly responsible for building Solomon's Temple and who was killed because he would not divulge certain secrets about its construction.

These are the three stages that are almost universal in Freemasonry throughout the world. Though there are other degrees, which differ from one Masonic body to another, almost all agree that these three specific ceremonies are what confer full membership upon a Mason.

There are great arguments within Freemasonry itself as to exactly what its origins may be. Few brothers doubt that Freemasonry developed from the guilds of the stonemasons but Grand Lodge in London, for example, doesn't specifically concern itself with what might have happened before its own creation in the eighteenth century. What remains a certainty is that Freemasonry certainly isn't an eighteenth-century phenomenon. Many Scottish Lodges, for example, trace their history to a point well before this time. Scottish records show that at least three lodges there date back to 1598 but this is merely the time at which they are first mentioned.

All Freemasonry is replete with symbolism, some of which is clearly very old in nature. Of course, this does not mean that Freemasonry itself has to be ancient. Modern druids, for example, meet annually at places like Stonehenge in England, to enact ceremonies that are supposed to be related to those of their Celtic counterparts of over two thousand years ago. However, modern druidism, like English Freemasonry, came into existence in the eighteenth century and probably has nothing at all to do with its genuine historical counterpart. Similarly with Freemasonry it has to be seen as at least a possibility that the trappings of the Craft have gradually been amassed from other sources and that the organization as a whole has no independent, ancient pedigree.

What is evident within Freemasonry, whether of ancient of more recent origin, is its astronomical and astrological heritage. This remains completely unknown to most brother Masons but I was first introduced to its significance thanks to a book published back in the nineteenth century. The book is entitled *Stellar Theology and Masonic Astronomy*. It was first published in 1882 and was written by an American Freemason called Robert Hewitt Brown.

Brown was obviously an accomplished astronomer and was also well versed in astrology. He took every symbol and ritual significant to Freemasonry and explained its astronomical and astrological significance. After reading the book carefully, bearing in mind my own background in astronomy and astrology, I was left in no doubt at all that there are matters at the heart of Freemasonic practice that are probably quite unknown to a large percentage of its membership. Even if this wealth of knowledge means nothing to the modern world it remains a fact that Freemasonry is definitely not what it appears – a simple fraternal gathering of like-minded individuals. In its symbols and practices it is most definitely based on genuine religious beliefs and physical observations of the cosmos that go back at least several thousand years.

It is certain that Robert Hewitt Brown was not the only Freemason who was of the opinion that its origins lay in ancient cosmology and mythology and I was intrigued to notice how the copy of his book that I had acquired had been deliberately defaced. The book I possess is a photocopy of the original work that is presently held in a famous Masonic library in the United States of America, though confidentiality prevents me from naming the actual source. As I read through the book I noticed that in various places the text had been deliberately defaced, most probably with pen and ink. Whole paragraphs had been obliterated in the original book but whoever had undertaken this exercise had worked in vain. The simple process of photocopying the book had, by a fortunate chance, made it possible, with some difficulty, to read the text that the censor had so carefully tried to hide.

Each and every paragraph and line that had been defaced dealt directly with either the Great Goddess of the ancients, or was related to the zodiac constellation of Virgo. Why had someone gone to this trouble to do this and what was it about these sections that this individual had not wished his brother Masons to see? The answer was self-evident because the sections in questions were those that suggested a strong religious bias at the heart of Freemasonry that was specifically associated with Goddess worship!

I intend to show that there is absolutely no doubt regarding the true religious imperatives of Freemasonry and there is no better place to start than with a symbol well known to all Freemasons who reach the third degree ceremony of Master Mason. This is the figure known as the "Beautiful Virgin."

CHAPTER FIVE

THE WEEPING VIRGIN

THE WEEPING VIRGIN

The Weeping Virgin of the Third Degree

The picture shown above is one of deep Freemasonic importance. It is associated with the third-degree ceremony of the Craft. This degree raises the aspirant to the full rank of Maser Mason and is, therefore, without argument, the most important ceremony within Freemasonry. What we see displayed in this picture is the Beautiful Virgin. She faces a broken column, she is weeping, and in her hand she has a sprig of acacia. Behind her stands what looks like Father Time and before her is displayed a part of the zodiac. Immediately above her head is an astrological glyph that denotes the zodiac sign of Virgo.

Ask a hundred knowledgeable Freemasons what any given symbol within the Craft is actually supposed to mean and there's a good chance you will get at least fifty different answers. This is certainly true with regard to what is alternatively known as "The Weeping Virgin" or "The Beautiful Virgin of the Third Degree." In fact, there is very little about this symbol on which Freemasons can comment with any degree of accuracy.

The most common explanation for the broken column is that it represents an epitaph to a character who is very important to Freemasonic ritual and mythology. His name is Hiram Abif and he is supposed to have been the man who was in charge of the building of Solomon's Temple in Jerusalem. History has left us no knowledge of such an individual but the Bible does say that Solomon sent to Tyre, because there wasn't anyone within his own domains who had sufficient skill to build the fantastic and ornate temple he required. The man who agreed to help with the job was in fact called Hiram, but Hiram of Tyre, not Hiram Abif.[1] What is more, Hiram of Tyre was a king and no mere architect or stonemason. Nevertheless, there may be a degree of truth in the story. Tyre was a Phoenician city and the Phoenicians were recognized builders and metal workers, which at the time the Hebrews were not. It is possible that the original name intended was "Huram abit," which means "Son of Hiram" and that not being understood, it gradually became corrupted.

The importance of Hiram Abif to Freemasonry lays not so much in his life, but rather the manner of his death. Masonic ritual says that the Temple was almost finished and that certain Masons sought out Hiram Abif, in order to obtain from him an important "secret" regarding the Temple. Hiram, who is referred to as the "son of the widow" refused on several occasions to reveal the secret, even when he was threatened with violence. Because he would not divulge this most important of secrets he was killed by the jealous workers. Immediately they had committed the deed they feared the retribution that would come upon them and they temporarily hid the body, marking the site of the shallow grave with a sprig of acacia.

In Masonic ritual their crime is reported to King Solomon, who sends out other workers to find Hiram and to bring back those responsible. The grave is

---

1 1 Kings 7.

discovered because the acacia has not taken root and comes out easily in the hands of one of those conducting the search. After a struggle with his putrefying flesh Hiram is raised from his grave, a feat that can only be accomplished with the right sort of "grip." Solomon is told that the villains have been apprehended and executed and all lament the passing in this awful way of such a virtuous and loyal man.

It is suggested that the broken column in the symbol of the weeping virgin is to commemorate Hiram Abif and that the sprig of acacia she carries is the same plant that marked his temporary grave. This story is fine as far as it goes but it isn't really much of an explanation at all. There is no beautiful virgin mentioned in the Hiram Abif legend, nor any column, broken or otherwise. Neither is the figure that looks like Father Time present in the story.

It is not particularly easy to discover exactly when the weeping virgin first became associated with Freemasonry. It was once thought that the virgin and the broken pillar had been introduced by an eminent American Freemason whose name was Jeremy Cross. Cross did indeed create a number of new hieroglyphs to be used in American Freemasonry. These, he suggested, would focus the mind of Masons on specific parts of their legends and rituals. Cross first published a picture of the broken column and the virgin in 1819. He guarded his hieroglyphs jealously and went to court on a number of occasions to retain his copyright on them, but whether this sort of action was justified in the case of the broken column and the virgin is in great doubt. He asserted that he had copied the broken column from a tomb in a graveyard in New York, which was the epitaph of a war hero, Commodore Lawrence. This may be true, but neither the broken column nor the virgin was his original invention.

A particular version of the third-degree ritual was known as the "Barney Ritual." This ritual, which certainly appeared as early as 1817, contained the marble column, the beautiful virgin, the sprig of acacia, and Father Time. The Barney Ritual, which was British and not American, existed at least two years and probably more before Jeremy Cross published his version of the broken column and weeping virgin in *The True Masonic Chart* in 1819.[2]

In fact, the weeping virgin and the broken column could be, and almost certainly are, far, far older than the nineteenth century, though it has to be remembered that even if Jeremy Cross had created the hieroglyph from scratch it had already been in general use in Freemasonry for over 25 years before the vision

---

2 Jeremy Cross, The True Masonic Chart, Publisher Unknown, New York, 1819.

of La Salette took place. However, most Masonic historians agree that the legacy of the weeping virgin is truly ancient, particularly in connection with the broken column. There is hardly any doubt that the historical counterpart for the beautiful virgin of Freemasonry is the Egyptian Goddess, Isis.

Isis was the most famous and important of all the Egyptian female deities. She was the wife of the God Osiris and is of extremely ancient origin. Isis began her career as a goddess of the moon and of the harvest. In the legend of Isis and Osiris, Osiris was murdered by the god Set by being sealed into a sarcophagus and then thrown into the River Nile. The coffin floated down the Nile and out to sea as far as the Phoenician city of Byblos, where it became trapped inside a growing tamarisk tree. So splendid was the tree that the King of Byblos used it for a pillar to support a new palace he was building. Isis traced the sarcophagus and, taking on human guise, she took a job as a maid to the Queen of Byblos and her daughters. Eventually she revealed her true identity, broke open the pillar, and rescued her husband. Unfortunately for Osiris he was discovered again by Set and this time was chopped into pieces. Once again Isis traveled the world, this time to locate the pieces of her husband's dismembered body and reconstruct them. Osiris became the God of the Dead and was particularly revered at the time of the Old Kingdom, though worship of Isis, as the Great Virgin Mother, extended well into Christian times in some parts of the world.

Whoever introduced the weeping virgin to Freemasonic symbolism and ritual can hardly have failed to understand what she actually represented. The presence of the broken pillar is the real giveaway, together with the fact that she is weeping, which was an attribute of Isis in terms of her devotion to Osiris. Isis was adored across the whole known world and revered as a great friend of humanity, the peerless wife and mother, and the giver of farming, and in particular wheat and barley to humanity.

Despite the fact that Isis was married to Osiris, and bore him a son, she was still referred to as a 'Virgin Goddess'. This is because in some of the stories that circulated in Egypt she inseminated herself in order to give birth to her son Horus. The phallus of Osiris was the only part of his body that she could not locate after his body had been torn apart and Isis fashioned a new one from beeswax. In Ancient Egypt one of the titles of Isis was "Virgin of the World." In her guise as the perpetual virgin Isis has much in common with deities from other pantheons, for example the Greek Demeter and Persephone. These goddesses were often depicted in a tripartite form, being at one and the same time the virgin, the mother, and the crone.

It is entirely appropriate that the Masonic hieroglyph of the weeping virgin, being representative of Isis, should be shown alongside the zodiac sign of Virgo. Not only has this zodiac sign always been dedicated to the sacred virgin, but the sun occupies the sign of Virgo at the time of year at which corn, the gift of the Goddess, is cut. But the analogy goes deeper than this and takes us into the realms of the dying and resurrected God of the Corn.

I am far from being the first to suggest that enshrined within Freemasonry are significant aspects of what were known as the "Mystery Religions." The most famous of these was the Mystery of Demeter, which existed well into Christian times in Greece.

The center of the Mystery religion of Demeter was in Athens and at Eleusis, Greece, a small settlement not far to the West. In Greek legend Demeter was the eternal mother and gave birth to a daughter whose name was Persephone. Persephone was stolen away one day by Pluto, God of the Underworld, who took her to his own deep, dark domains. Demeter was distraught and spent a long time searching for Persephone, eventually tracing her to Hades. Demeter begged Zeus, king of the gods, to allow Persephone to be released and Zeus agreed, provided that Persephone had eaten nothing during her stay with Pluto. Unfortunately she had been tricked into eating one pomegranate seed. Zeus decreed that henceforth Persephone could spend two thirds of each year above, in the sunshine, and one third with her husband, Pluto, in the Underworld.

Demeter was responsible for climate and all growing things. The Greeks suggested that it was because of her distraction and sorrow while her daughter was away that nature died back during the winter. However, when Persephone is released from her bondage in the spring each year, Demeter is overwhelmed with joy and nature's bounty flourishes again.

Demeter is also associated with a god by the name of Dionysus. Dionysus is remembered as being the god of the vine and of the peaceful arts. He was born of Zeus and a mortal woman and in the very earliest legends probably had little or nothing to do with Demeter. In time he became her son, or even her husband in some stories, which differ from age to age and region to region throughout Greece. There was also a strong association between Persephone and Dionysus because both were absent during Demeter's grief, which led to the onset of winter. But while Persephone was merely transported to Hades each year, Dionysus was annually killed. The nature of his yearly death was gruesome because his body was chopped into pieces, boiled, roasted, and consumed. Each spring, some said thanks to the intervention of Demeter, Dionysus was born again, nature flourished, and the vines bore fruit.

The power of the cult of Dionysus cannot be overstated. His followers, usually women, held orgiastic ceremonies all over Greece and often carried small baskets on their head containing a phallus made from fig wood.

Nobody knows how early the association took place but there is no doubt that the cult of Dionysus became closely involved with that of Demeter. Some modern experts believe that the Mysteries of Demeter actually came from the island of Crete and had first been celebrated there by Europe's first super-civilization, the Minoans, possibly as early as 2000 BC.

The very reason we don't know more about the Mysteries of Demeter or what actually took place in Eleusis is precisely because they were "mysteries." Those taking part in the annual celebration were sworn to secrecy on pain of death. So effective were the penalties meted out that not one absolute account of the actual mystery survives. Nevertheless, we do have a fairly good idea what took place because Demeter's Mystery is broadly similar to other mystery cults that existed elsewhere in the ancient world.

Would-be aspirants of the cult would gather in Athens. In fact, there were two gatherings each year. The first, known as the "lesser mystery" was in the spring but this took place in Athens, and not at Eleusis itself. During the lesser mystery, aspirants were prepared and the ritual sacrifice of pigs took place. The real mystery was enacted in September when a huge procession left Athens and walked the 22 kilometers to Eleusis. So important was the great Mystery of Demeter that even wars would be suspended in order to allow for its celebration.

On 14 September certain ritual objects were brought from Eleusis to Athens, in preparation for the procession. On 16 September the initiates went together to Phaleron, to purify themselves in the sea there. On 17 September sacrifices were made at the Eleusinion, the temple dedicated to Demeter in Athens. Finally, on 19 September the procession to Eleusis took place and the celebration of the mysteries had truly begun. (In case the penny hasn't dropped, 19 September was the date of the La Salette vision.)

Although specific details of the ceremony that took place at Eleusis do not exist it is known that initiates went through a ceremony of "death and rebirth." It is suggested that there was a Gnostic element to the proceedings because the symbolic rebirth involved being incarnated not only into oneself but also into the Great Spirit that was all of creation. It is also known that the ceremony involved the eating of specially baked and sanctified barley cakes. There have been suggestions that these cakes may have been laced with some sort of mild hallucinogenic drug, which under the right suggestion from the priests would make the whole experience more magical and memorable.

The one aspect of the Mystery of Demeter that is certain is that of the ritual death and rebirth, which symbolically resonated with the story of Dionysus, who himself represented the grain from the fields and the fruits of nature that were annually "cut down or killed" so that humanity might eat. In this sense Dionysus represents a figure that occurred in many cultures – the dying and reborn corn god. Similar ceremonies also took place in the Mysteries of Isis, surrounding the ritual killing and resurrection of Osiris. Most of the European mysteries of the death and rebirth of nature seem to have originated in Crete, though that of Isis became "Helenized" in later Egyptian history and ultimately the worship of Isis was almost indistinguishable from that of Demeter.

In the figure of the Beautiful Virgin from the Freemasonic Third Degree we see a definite representation of this Demeter/Isis figure. There can be no doubt about this because whoever did create this hieroglyph has left us all the clues we need. First of all we can observe that the head of the young woman points directly at the zodiac sign of Virgo. This is a strong indication that she represents the Goddess who has, for thousands of years, been associated with the zodiac constellation that bears her name. In her right hand she holds up a sprig of acacia. In all probability this was originally the same ear of wheat that is usually held in pictures representing Virgo itself. Certainly the plant she holds in her left hand is vegetation of some sort and she holds it upon the part of the zodiac in which the sun is to be found at harvest time.

Her right hand is placed on the broken column, which is at one and the same time representative of death and also relates to the story of Isis and Osiris. The virgin weeps for the death of her consort, the corn god, who dies annually at this time of year so that humanity can eat. Father Time stands behind her, in an attitude of blessing – an assurance that with the passing of time the corn will grow again; in other words the god will be brought to birth once more and grow to be the consort of the Goddess.

I recently gave a talk to a large group of Scottish Freemasons and during the course of the evening I made mention of the Beautiful Virgin of the Third Degree and asked those present what they thought it meant to Freemasons. I was told that it exists to remind Freemasons to remember the integrity, sacrifice, and death of Hiram Abif but they had no idea as to the astrological component of the hieroglyph, except to suggest that this merely meant that the woman in question must be a virgin. The broken pillar, they had been told, was simply an epitaph to a great man who had been the first Grand Master of Freemasonry.

The parallels between the Beautiful Virgin of the Third Degree and the Virgin Mary in her guise as Our Lady of Sorrows seems too obvious to be nothing more than a coincidence. We know that the Mysteries of Demeter took place in September, at the time of the harvest, and we are certain that Dionysus and Osiris were both emblematic of a character that seems to have been around as long as religious belief has existed – the dying and reborn corn god. He was, for example, particularly relevant to the religious beliefs of the Minoans, Europe's first super-civilization that reached its height on the Island of Crete as early as 2000 BC. We might suppose, with some justification, that the dying and reborn corn god is, together with the Great Goddess, a remnant of a religious imperative that was widespread and that is certainly as old as farming, which commenced around 8000 BC.

It is also a fact that the feast of Our Lady of Sorrows takes place in September, at the very same time of year as the Mysteries of Demeter were held. Like Isis and Demeter, the Virgin Mary as Our Lady of Sorrows is crying for the death of her son, a son whom we will presently show was also, at least figuratively, her husband. We should also remember that the Virgin Mary who appeared at La Salette talked mostly to the two children who saw her there specifically about the harvest and the lack of respect people had for her own sacrifice and that of her son.

Freemasonry could be a composite of different ancient beliefs and knowledge, brought together like some strange cocktail three or more centuries ago, or it may be the genuine repository of a cohesive belief pattern that has somehow managed to survive, against all odds, for several thousand years. Either way, it is clearly very much more than a simple social club filled with meaningless gobbledygook. The deliberate eradication of text from a book specifically researched and written to show the ancient nature of Freemasonic ritual is very telling. This cannot have taken place before the late nineteenth century, because that is when the book was written. This means that someone, probably as recently as the first part of the twentieth century, was well aware of the elements of Goddess worship that exist at the heart of Freemasonry and wished to keep it from his fellows.

If Freemasons were responsible for the vision at La Salette, they were clearly equating the Virgin Mary with the ancient deity that lies at the heart of their own organization. We should not forget that every man raised to the third degree undergoes the same ritual death and rebirth that lies at the heart of the Demeter Mysteries and which epitomizes the stories of Isis and Osiris and those of Demeter and Dionysus. Each one of them becomes, in a figurative sense, the dying and reborn god of the corn, the alter ego of the mythical Hiram Abif.

Despite these connections we could be forgiven for thinking that Freemasonry does seem to be a fairly modern invention because we hear nothing substantial about it until the sixteenth century, which in terms of humanity's existence might as well be yesterday. Is it therefore possible that Freemasonry could be simply the latest manifestation of something very much older? If so, can we work backwards in time to establish its parentage? In fact we can. It's a long journey and our starting point must be an important meeting that was held in Anatolia in AD 325.

Chapter Six

Into the Melting Pot

INTO THE MELTING POT

By the early fourth century the Roman Empire was suffering from significant problems. A combination of infighting between would-be emperors and incursions across its borders from barbarian outsiders was taking its toll. The great days of the Claudian emperors were long gone and the empire was starting on the long, slippery slope towards collapse. However, a temporary respite did come along in 306 when a man of great energy and intelligence was proclaimed emperor. His name was Constantine.

Constantine was born around AD 285, the son of Constantius Chlorus, one of several men who were running the Roman Empire at the time. When Constantius died in York in 306 Constantine was present and his enthusiastic troops proclaimed him the new emperor. What followed was a long period of bitter fighting as Constantine struggled to secure his position against rivals. It was not until October of 312, with a final victory at the Milvian Bridge in Italy, that his position was safe and the new emperor could turn his mind to securing peace in the empire as a whole.

Constantine knew all too well that the vast Roman Empire lacked cohesion and it became his aim to find ways to cement the many factions and nations together. One way this might be achieved would be through commonality, particularly in terms of religion. The empire was composed of hundreds of linguistic groups with different historical and religious backgrounds. Then, as now, religion was a prime cause of civil unrest and Constantine seems to have decided that a single, cohesive belief pattern for his many disparate subjects would solve at least some of his problems.

The difficulty that he faced was in deciding which of the many religions on offer throughout the Roman Empire he should choose. There were many contenders. The gods of the old Roman pantheon were still worshiped across a large area, though the Egyptian cult of Isis had become tremendously important, even thousands of miles from the cities on the Nile. Greek influences were also extremely strong. In the East, Zoroastrianism was popular, while the troops of the army were turning in ever-greater numbers towards an offshoot of Zoroastrianism, which worshiped a solar deity named Mithra. In the end, Constantine seems to have decided on a compromise that might prove acceptable to the greatest number of his subjects and went for a belief pattern that had originated in Palestine three centuries before and which, even though persecuted by previous emperors, showed no signs of diminishing in popularity. Constantine chose Christianity to be the accepted religion across the Roman Empire.

There are probably many reasons why Constantine took this decision. Certainly Christianity was not his own preferred belief. He was an enthusiastic worshiper of Mithra, as were large numbers of his generals and soldiers. But this was not be too much of a problem because by the fourth century there already seems to have been a significant fusion of Christian and Mithraic beliefs. Constantine could highlight these in order to make the resulting religion acceptable to as many people as possible.

Before the emperor could hope to establish Christianity across the empire, he first had to establish exactly what it represented. In the period between the death of its supposed founder, Jesus ben Joseph, a prophet and some said a god from Galilee, Christians had broken into a number of different sects. In fact, this was a process that had begun almost as soon as the belief began to gain ground. There were two main factions to consider. One group, the Arianists, named after their leader Arius, claimed that Jesus had been a "creation" of God, which in effect made him a prophet. The other contending party held to the line that Jesus was "one" with God as part of a mystical trinity that was seen as the Father, the Son, and the Holy Spirit.

It isn't hard to see how Constantine's vote would be cast. He had worshiped Mithra all his life. Mithra was already recognized as having sprung from God, though without being in any way inferior to him. He was, to all intents and purposes, the same as God. The Emperor must have realized that there were such definite similarities between Christianity and Mithraism that if he played his cards right, he could please almost everyone – and most specifically his soldiers, upon whose shoulders the safety of the empire rested.

In 325 a great gathering was arranged in Anatolia, at a city called Nicea. There, Constantine assembled the leaders of the different Christian denominations and instructed them that Christianity would become the preferred religion of the Roman Empire. The only slight fly in the ointment was that there could be only "one" form of Christianity, which he would have to personally approve.

From the word go the Arianists were out in the cold. They were told that unless they accepted that Jesus and God were one and the same thing, they would henceforth be considered heretics and would be persecuted with all the zeal that had come upon Christians as a whole until only a few decades before. What emerged from Nicea was, in reality, a new religion, synthesized from Christianity, with overlays of Mithraism and the Mystery religions that had emanated from Egypt and especially Greece. With just a little flexibility all round it would be possible for almost everyone to find something recognizable within the new religion and it might just represent the glue necessary to hold the empire together during difficult times.

Constantine must surely have been delighted with the result, not least because it hardly changed his own religious preference at all. Mithra had been born in a stable of a virgin mother and had appeared in the world as a human being. Mithra had been tortured and murdered and after three days he had risen from the dead. Almost identical stories had now become attached to Jesus and a little judicious editing of the documents pertaining to Christianity would make the fusion even tighter. The two religions were fairly similar in terms of age, with Mithraism probably the older of the two, having sprung from ancient Persian beliefs. (In times to come the Christian Church would say that the similarities between Christianity and Mithraism were the work of the Devil, who had deceived true Christian believers by placing the legends of Mithra in the historical record prior to Christ's birth!)

Christianity truly had something for everyone and its most ingenious slant was that it harped back to a commonality with ancient religion that would prove imperative to its success. Both Jesus and Mithra could be seen as examples of the ancient dying and resurrected god of the corn. In the case of Christianity this connection was made explicit by the words of Jesus immediately prior to his death and rebirth. Whether or not Jesus actually uttered these words is open to debate but the gospels give us an account of the Last Supper. In Matthew 26:26 we read:

> And as they were eating, Jesus took bread, and blessed it, and broke it, and gave it to the disciples, and said, "Take, eat; this is my body."

Then in, again in Matthew 26:27 we have:

> And he took the cup, and gave thanks, and gave it to them, saying, "Drink ye all of it; For this is my blood of the new testament, which is shed for many for the remission of sins."

There can be no more explicit proof of Jesus' position as the corn god than these utterances, either because this was a connection he deliberately made himself, or because words were subsequently put into his mouth.

There were other aspects of Christianity that would prove to be popular across many borders. Those who still held to a belief in a female deity, of which there must have been many hundreds of thousands, could find solace in the character of the Virgin Mary. Even by the time of Nicea, Mary was being referred to as "Theotokus," the "God Bearer." Although in centuries to come her position within Christianity would fluctuate, at the time of the formalization of Christianity she could clearly be equated with Isis, Demeter, and a host of other local goddesses across the empire.

Thus, what had originally been a very local "schism" within Judaism, was turned into a "cure-all" religion that would, at least temporarily, help to rescue an ailing empire. Nevertheless, the writing was already on the wall and by the fifth century the pressures upon Rome were so great that legions guarding the extremities of the empire had to be recalled. Britain suffered as a result, and so did the area we now call France, which to the Romans was known as Gaul.

By the middle of the fifth century Gaul was left to defend itself, which, without the legions, it clearly had no chance of doing. The resulting vacuum was filled by Frankish tribes from across the Rhine. These first invaders were Salian Franks and specifically a people who knew themselves as the Merovingians. They claimed descent from a semi-mythical character by the name of Merovee but also suggested that they had originally represented a sect of Judaism. They claimed to have fled the Near East when the tribe of Benjamin had been attacked by other Hebrew tribes and had found refuge in parts of Greece, specifically in Troy. Because of this they named one of their first major cities in Northern Gaul "Troyes" after their supposed Greek homeland.

The greatest leader of the Merovingians was Clovis (456–511). He occupied Northern Gaul in 486 and gradually increased his power and influence in order to conquer much of the geographical area of modern France. The Merovingians were not Christian until 496, at which time Clovis accepted baptism. Why he took this step is not really known. It may have been a result of the same sort of political expediency that had attended the conversion of Constantine over a century earlier. Certainly by taking this action Clovis allied himself with Rome, which would have been a satisfactory state of affairs for a leader anxious to protect his Southern and Eastern borders.

A great percentage of Clovis' subjects followed his lead, but in order to convert the mass of the Franks, missionaries had to be brought from elsewhere and we know that the majority of these came from Britain and Ireland. Although we tend to think of the Roman Catholic Church as having held supremacy across all of Europe, no such cohesive institution existed at the time. Christianity during this period, although owing some loyalty to Rome, was actually a very local affair. Services, forms of worship, and even religious dates remained peculiar to different regions. The Christians predominating in Britain and Ireland at the time were known as "Culdees." The priests of the Culdees had much in common with the old Bardic and Druidic traditions of both Britain and Gaul. The Christianity of the Culdees was heavily affected by pre-Christian beliefs, with a strong element of nature worship and a fierce sense of independence that would not be relinquished lightly. It is almost certainly within the heady mixture of religion from the Far West, together with the supposed Judaic/Greek origins of the Merovingians, that a definite schism within Christianity began to ferment in Northern France during the sixth century.

The established Church in Rome was so pleased with the conversion of Clovis and his subjects that it formed a pact with him, promising that he and his successors would hold a very special place as Christian kings. Unfortunately for the Merovingians the promises that came from Rome weren't worth a great deal. As was the tradition with the Franks, when Clovis died, his extensive kingdoms were divided among his sons and with this act the seeds of the fall of the Merovingian dynasty were planted.

Several generations and a great deal of infighting later, a young king by the name of Dagobert II came to the throne of Austrasia, which was part of the old kingdom carved out by Clovis. Dagobert was the son of Sigebert, who died in 656 while Dagobert was a child. In danger of his life because of factions within the court, Dagobert was sent to Ireland and then England to be educated. He was therefore brought up in the ways of the Culdees, with their peculiar form of Christianity. On returning to France to take his throne, Dagobert was treacherously murdered in the Forest of Stennay in 679. From this point on Merovingian kings were puppets, subject to the will of a group of high-ranking civil servants who were known as "The Mayors of the Palace."

By 714, any pretence that the Mayors were only the political front men for the Merovingian monarchs was dispelled when one of their number, Pepin the Short, was crowned King of the Franks. His coronation was accepted and even welcomed by the Church in Rome and so its special connection with the

Merovingians came to an abrupt end. Pepin was the first of a dynasty of kings who are known to us as the Carolingians. There is no doubt at all that a large group of people within France saw the actions of the Church as being treacherous in the extreme. Support for the Merovingian cause remained in place for centuries and it was almost certainly from this point in time that direct opposition to the established Catholic Church began to ferment in two adjacent regions of Northern France, Champagne and Burgundy. It is also obvious that there were radical differences in religious belief existing in these regions. It is quite possible that there had been strong early influence from a charismatic Jewish sect known as the Essene, which had flourished in Palestine around the time of Jesus. The Greek past of the Merovingians seems to have given them a particular reverence for the Mystery religion of Demeter. In addition the region had formerly been very responsive to a powerful female deity by the name of Rosemerth.

As the Carolingians gradually gained power, the dynasty gave birth to the greatest of its kings. Charlemagne was born in 742 and took the throne in 771. Two years later he received a plea from the Pope, Hadrian II, to come to the aid of the Vatican because Italy was under attack from the Lombards, who were invading the Papal States. Charlemagne responded and although he freed Rome from the Lombards, he insisted that he be proclaimed "Protector of the Church." In effect he was the first Holy Roman Emperor.

From this point on the Church did not control the Carolingians, they controlled it. This was fortuitous because at the same time they were introducing a radically different form of government from that of the Merovingians. Clovis had been content to rely on the sort of administration that had been employed in Gaul by Rome but the Carolingians introduced feudalism.

Feudalism introduced a form of government and society that can be viewed as a sort of pyramid. At the top sits the king, and everyone below him is subservient to his whims. Below the king are great landowners, who also have private armies. They, like everyone else, derive their power from the king and owe loyalty to him, especially in times of war. Below the great barons are the middle-ranking aristocracy, who owe fealty to those above them and ultimately to the king. When armed struggle is necessary they provide soldiers to fight from the great barons.

Further down the pyramid we find the local lords, who owe fealty to the middle-ranking aristocrats and at the bottom of the pyramid we find the freemen, serfs, and finally the slaves. The vast majority of the people in feudal Western Europe were serfs. They owned nothing, though they had land from their lord that they were allowed to cultivate. As tribute they also ploughed, planted, and harvested the lord's land. Serfs were not free to come and go as they pleased and were only very slightly better off than the slaves, who had absolutely no rights at all.

This form of government clearly went down very badly with the remnants of the Merovingian Franks. What made matters worse was the fact that Charlemagne now had possession of the Church, which he and his successors fought hard to make into an instrument that would serve the feudal State well. Henceforth all services, throughout the Catholic world, would be spoken in Latin. They would all follow a specific form and no room for local deviation was allowed. So powerful was Charlemagne that it would have been impossible for the Merovingians to stage any sort of armed rebellion, but what happened subsequently demonstrates that moves were being made to remedy the situation in other ways.

These actions were being taken by the middle-ranking aristocrats located in Champagne and Burgundy. Their view of both society and religion was wildly at odds with that of the Carolingians and although they could do nothing to bring about immediate change, we can be certain that they were already beginning to make subtle moves, even while Charlemagne was in power. It is with these peculiar and heretical families in Northern and Central France that we find the first real evidence of what would eventually lead to Freemasonry. Their objectives were fuelled by a fierce independence, a hatred of oppression in any form, and a specific reverence for forms of worship that could only be loosely allied to the kind of Christianity that existed in Rome.

Instead of pointlessly rebelling and trying to defeat the Carolingians by force of arms, they turned instead to subterfuge – a policy that they and their descendants would follow for many centuries. They were very patient and were clearly willing to wait a long time to achieve their objectives. It is clear that they started to take action as early as the ninth century but their first cohesive effort to subvert both Church and State came in the form of a series of multi-pronged actions that commenced toward the end of the eleventh century.

CHAPTER SEVEN

THE QUIET REVOLUTION

THE QUIET REVOLUTION

What was gradually taking place in Champagne and Northern Burgundy between the eighth and the eleventh centuries was the fermentation of what was probably the greatest conspiracy the world would ever know. It required decades of careful planning among aristocratic families that must have appeared to the outside world to be contributing fully to the society of which they were a part. However, it can be shown that this was not the case at all, because when the time came, this group of heretics and would-be political reformers was ready with a raft of moves that would change the face of Europe, and ultimately the world, for ever.

The first action in this multi-pronged plan was to secure the Vatican. This eventually became possible in the form of Odo of Lagery. Odo was born of an aristocratic family in Châtillon-sur-Marne, near Troyes in Champagne. This cardinal, blood-tied to the counts of Champagne, had served long and hard under the two previous Popes, Gregory the Great and Victor III, and was elected Pope himself in 1088 at the relatively tender age of 46. The election of Odo, who took the name Urban II, marked the right time to begin putting a whole series of other plans into action. The first of these was to persuade the new Pope to preach for a Crusade to gain Jerusalem for Christianity. Even this probably wasn't necessary because it is entirely likely that he had been placed in the path of the Vatican throne with this explicit purpose in mind.

On 27 November, at Clermont in France, Urban II called for the combined forces of Christendom to unite in a Holy War that would free the Holy Land from Muslim domination. Even aside from the obvious association Urban had with the planners in Champagne, the Crusade must have seemed expedient to him. For one thing it would rid the West for a while at least of the younger sons of the aristocracy, who, fully armed, aggressive, and keen to fight anyone, were causing problems, even for the Church. In addition, there would be significant kudos for any Pope who was responsible for putting Jerusalem into Christian hands – but there were potential problems too and these might have stayed the arm of any pontiff other than one hand-picked by the heretics of Champagne.

What seems to have interested the Champagne heretics, almost beyond anything else, was the establishment of a New Jerusalem. This was much more than the liberation of the city itself. It was nothing less than a religious and political ideal that served a wealth of different purposes.

With Jerusalem in Christian hands, the importance of Rome as the ecclesiastical center of Christendom would surely diminish. After all, Jesus had been born, served his ministry, and died in the Near East. Jerusalem was the holiest city in the world. If the area could be wrested from the grip of the Muslims and made permanently safe, Rome might be abandoned in favor of Jerusalem and the influence of the Church as an arm of the State may well be diminished. The "New Jerusalem" was also a political ideal but one that could be justified by Scripture. It was mentioned in the Book of Revelations, a most extraordinary work tacked onto the New Testament, a tract that was of tremendous importance at this time. Less well known in this period was the fact that the establishment of a New Jerusalem had first been mooted as the prime objective of a strange and enigmatic branch of Judaism known as the Essene.

The Essene had lived in desert communities along the Jordan Valley, but had also enjoyed significant influence in Jerusalem. They had flourished around the time of Jesus and it has been suggested by numerous scholars that Jesus himself, together with John the Baptist, may have been directly associated with this enigmatic group. What the Essene seem to have represented was a sort of monastic community, but one with every intention of becoming a powerful army. The enemy they sought to fight had not been Muslims, because that religion had not yet arisen. Rather, they wished to throw off the yoke of the Roman forces that occupied their country, and in particular their capital of Jerusalem.

The Essene created libraries of scrolls, many of which were found during the 1940s, hidden in caves near Qumran, close to the River Jordan, where one of the Essene communities had been established. The scrolls included elaborate plans for raising, training, and arming a huge army. The documents do not make it clear that the perceived enemy was the Roman legions, but there seems to be very little doubt that the Essene intention was to defeat the Romans once and for all and to liberate their land. Things probably got out of hand too soon because in AD 70 the Jews in Palestine did revolt against Roman occupation – a revolt that was quelled with the utmost ferocity and massive loss of life. In the ensuing carnage the Essene disappeared from history, though it is my profound belief that they were not all slaughtered. As we shall see, some of the actions of the heretics of Champagne would have close parallels with Essene beliefs and actions. The Essene were, at best, a very strange branch of Judaism. They kept a solar rather than a lunar calendar, were monastic in nature and celibate (both anachronisms to Jews) and they had strange forms of worship that involved a great deal of ritual bathing.

Early Christian leaders, such as Augustine of Hippo (354–430) and the later St Benedict of Nursia (480–547) had both drawn attention to the creation of a New Jerusalem. To these holy men of the Church, the contemplation had been of a spiritual paradise – a place to which God would return and judge the righteous, but to the Champagne plotters the New Jerusalem would be far less spiritual and a great deal more practical. It was, in fact, more in line with the intentions of the Essene.

Soldiers came from all over Europe and beyond gradually made their way to the Holy Land. Jerusalem was eventually surrounded and fell to the forces of the Crusaders in 1099. First over the broken walls was Godfroi de Bouillon, a French noble with strong Merovingian blood in his veins. By his side were the Count of Champagne and a man who would become important a few years later – a vassal of the Count of Champagne named Hughes de Payen.

As the Crusading armies had taken up their positions in the Levant in 1098, another part of the plan was taking shape. Robert de Molesmes, also a native of Troyes in Champagne, together with a handful of his followers, was founding not only a new abbey but a whole new form of monasticism. Robert was the son of a high-ranking Champagne family and had been a monk from a very early age. He was a staunch reformer of the Benedictine Order and had twice created new abbeys, but after each attempt the new foundation had become lax and lazy. Travelling to land given to him by the Count of Burgundy, Robert went to a place near Dijon that would eventually come to be known as Citeaux. There the Cistercian Order of Monks came into being, sanctioned by the Pope soon after their arrival at Citeaux.

The Cistercians were an important part of the Champagne strategy because they were much more than simply another group of monks. After what seemed like a somewhat faltering start in Citeaux, the Order began to spread exponentially across Europe and beyond, though not with any great speed before the arrival of an Englishman named Stephen Harding and a man of ultimately Champagne origin called Bernard.

Stephen Harding was important because it was he who would pen the Rules of the new Order, which would be quite different from those of any other monastic institution. Bernard arrived at Citeaux in 1113, three years after Stephen Harding, with a large collection of relatives and friends, declaring his intention of becoming a Cistercian monk. In the greater scheme of things there was nothing remotely coincidental about this state of affairs. Bernard would go down in history of St Bernard of Clairvaux and he ranks as one of the most important men in the whole of European history.

Bernard was the son of Tescellin, Lord of Fontainnes, near Dijon in Northern Burgundy, and his mother was Aleth of Montbard, the daughter of an influential family from Champagne. Tescellin had fought with distinction alongside Godfroi de Bouillon and the Count of Champagne at Jerusalem and had been present during the storming of the city. Bernard's mother, Aleth, was blood-tied to the Counts of Champagne, which made Bernard a cousin to the count himself. Bernard served only three years at Citeaux before he was despatched to form his own abbey. This was at Clairvaux, immediately adjacent to Troyes, capital of Champagne. St Bernard of Clairvaux is still revered as being among the greatest of Catholics and is revered as a "Doctor" of the Church, yet his actions and his obvious beliefs make this extremely odd.

ABOUT THE CISTERCIANS

No group of religious adherents can claim to have had more of a bearing on the history of Europe and the world than that of the Cistercians. From the outset of their existence they showed themselves to be radically different than anything that had gone before and they became the most successful monastic order that has ever existed in the world. On the surface, they represented a reformed version of the Benedictine Order, but they differed radically in many ways from their predecessors.

The Cistercians immediately became known as the "white monks" because they wore habits of bleached sheep's wool. They lived an austere life and specialized in taking on marginal land that nobody else coveted. Once granted access to such holdings they would soon build a rudimentary abbey and begin farming.

What immediately set the Cistercians apart was their commitment to hard manual work, and the way they organized their communities. Another difference between them and the Benedictines is that the Cistercians enrolled two types of monk. The first group, choir monks, were generally ordained priests. In addition to many daily church services they were expected to do their share of manual work but they rarely if ever left the precincts of the abbey. In addition, the Cistercians formed a second tier of monks, known as lay brothers. These men were not ordained priests, though they took vows of poverty and chastity as did the choir monks. The real difference lay in the fact that the lay brothers were able to live away from the confines of the abbey, often in remote farms known as granges. They also attended regular worship but their primary function was a practical one.

The Cistercian abbeys were essentially a series of democratic communities, living as islands within deeply feudal societies. All choir monks met at chapter each day, where the business of the abbey was decided. It was at chapter that new abbots were elected, together with other officers of the house. This was done by democratic vote from which no choir monk was excluded. The same democracy existed further up the Cistercian family tree. Each elected abbot traveled at least once a year to Citeaux, there to sit in chapter for the whole Order. When a vacancy arose, the leader of the Order was chosen by the abbots of all the other Cistercian houses and just as in the case of abbots, he could be removed by their vote if it was deemed necessary.

When a particular abbey started to become successful, which didn't usually take long with grants of land and money coming in from an enthusiastic public, a group of twelve monks would set off to found a new abbey. This would then become a daughter house of the one from which it had been founded. This is essentially how the Order spread exponentially, with many daughter houses eventually spawning daughter houses of their own.

Cistercian communities were very self-sufficient but where specialized trades were concerned, a particular abbey might provide what other abbeys needed, as well as selling their goods into the open market. One Cistercian house might mine and smelt lead, which would be sent to roof the naves of sister houses, while another would specialize in making carts. All the Cistercian abbeys were models of efficiency – all had smithies and forges, tanneries and brew-houses. But by far and away the greatest success of the Cistercian monasteries, particularly the ones in Britain, lay in sheep rearing and wool production.

It was the policy of the Cistercians to grab whatever land they could in a particular district, no matter how far away from the abbey it might be. Then by swapping, buying, and extorting if necessary, they welded their disparate plots together to create huge granges. In an era when most farming was managed on crudely arranged and wasteful village strips, the Cistercian methods were positively revolutionary. Even after their own demise the efforts of the Cistercians would give the greatest impetus to the Agricultural Revolution that would precede industrialization in Britain by the seventeenth century.

Abbeys such as Rievaulx and Fountains in Yorkshire, England, eventually had thousands of head of sheep and were exporting massive amounts of wool each year. All of the wool was sheared and sorted by the monks themselves and the profits were dazzling.

The similarities between the Cistercians and the Essene brotherhood of the Jordan Valley were noteworthy, even though the two institutions were separated by over a thousand years. The Essene had also chosen to wear white and they practiced self-sufficiency. Like the Cistercians, they had lay brothers, or "lesser" brothers, and they worshiped at prescribed times throughout each day.

The Essene were famous for their ritual bathing. Large baths have been excavated at Qumran and at other Essene sites. To a slightly lesser extent this was also true of the Cistercians, who, at a time when bathing of any sort was very much frowned upon, were expected to wash every day and to keep themselves generally clean. Faucets were supplied at every Cistercian abbey for this specific purpose. Also like the Essene, the Cistercians refrained from building their abbeys near to existing communities. They chose to live, as St Bernard said, "in deserts" and though these were not the same sort of desert to be found in the Jordan Valley, they were desolate places nonetheless.

Both organizations looked towards the New Jerusalem and both were associated with a powerful fighting brotherhood, even though in the case of the Essene this never seems to have become a reality.

The Cistercians soon became expert builders. They had to because their Order was spreading so quickly. What is of particular note is the fact that they set up colleges of stonemasons. One such existed near the Cistercian abbey of Melrose in Scotland. Cistercian architecture was, at first, extremely plain, with little or no ornamentation. Parts of abbeys were prefabricated and then taken to the requisite site and most of the abbeys had a similar form. It was said that a blind Cistercian choir monk from Scotland would have no difficulty finding his way around a strange Cistercian house in Italy because the arrangement of its buildings would be so familiar. In the end there were well over 500 Cistercian abbeys, from Wales in the West to Palestine in the East.

Cistercian abbeys were a combination of churches, living accommodation, and factories. Always based on rivers, or artificial canals dug for the purpose, they were clean, hygienic, and laid out so as to allow numerous processes to take place. Cistercians were also innovative. They employed water power for numerous purposes and improved technology wherever they could. Archaeologists at Rievaulx Abbey in Yorkshire claim to have excavated what looks like the world's very first blast furnace for making steel, two centuries ahead of their appearance elsewhere in Britain. Cistercians mined coal, smelted metals of all kinds, and led the field in providing medical care to their own brethren.

In a religious sense the Cistercians were virtually obsessed with the Virgin Mary. Each and every abbey was named for her and she was deeply venerated at every service, of which there were many each day. However, nobody in the Cistercian Order was more dedicated to the Virgin than the most famous Cistercian of them all – St Bernard of Clairvaux.

ST BERNARD OF CLAIRVAUX

Bernard of Clairvaux was never the head of the Cistercian Order, but this can only be because he preferred not to accept the position. He could easily have been elected Pope if he had chosen to stand for the office. For most of his adult life his word was law in the Cistercian communities everywhere and also within the Church as a whole. Bernard claimed to have had a mystical experience early in his career. He was worshiping before the statue of the Madonna when the statue lifted her hand to her breast. Drops of milk dripped from the Madonna's breast and fell into Bernard's open mouth. From this moment on St Bernard dedicated his life to her service. He penned dozens of sermons based around a strange, pagan-sounding little book from the Old Testament, known as "Solomon's Song of Songs." This deals with a bride and bridegroom. Bernard was a mystic and equated the bride in the Song of Songs with the Virgin, whom he saw as the bride of Christ.

St Bernard became very influential during his life. He "made" Popes and admonished them if they did not come up to his standards. Neither was he above criticizing those of aristocratic or even royal blood. He was also very responsive to the needs of Jews, despite the fact that they were deeply marginalized by Catholic communities across Europe at the time. On occasion he would walk many miles to quell pogroms or to settle disputes that looked like causing problems for Jewish communities. Bernard was fascinated by building and was primarily responsible for setting up the colleges of stonemasons established by the Cistercians. His personal faith was strange and quite Culdean in nature and he once referred to God as being "height and breadth and depth and length." He also maintained that one could find God more readily in nature than in any church.

Constantly keeping cordial relations with his kin in nearby Troyes, St Bernard traveled much but always returned to his own abbey of Clairvaux. Its name literally meant "Valley of Clear Sight" but it was built in a place that had formerly been known as Vallee d'Absinthe, because a bitter herb had grown there in profusion. Another name for absinthe is wormwood, which is also the name given to a comet in the Book of Revelations, the arrival of which, Revelation claims, would help to create the havoc that will be the precursor to the establishment of the New Jerusalem.

There can be no doubt that St Bernard of Clairvaux was closely involved with the heretic movement that was proving to be so successful in Champagne and Burgundy during his life. He had been placed in the center of the Cistercian movement for specific purposes and proved to be an able general in all matters. Probably his most decisive move, and the one that would have the most profound bearing on the future, was his championing of an offshoot of the Cistercian Order that would come to be known as the Knights Templar.

CHAPTER EIGHT

THE JERUSALEM CONNECTION

The Jerusalem Connection

Three years after Bernard took control of his own abbey at Clairvaux, a group of knights set off from Champagne to Jerusalem. They were nine in number and at least three of them were related to Bernard. All were knights and from at least middle-ranking aristocratic families. Their leader was Hugh de Payen, a man who held lands in Troyes and who was the vassal of Hugh, the Count of Champagne. Contemporary accounts suggest that the purpose of this journey was for the knights to guard the roads from the shores of Palestine so that pilgrims could visit the holy sites in the Levant. This is patently absurd for such a small group and in any case they did nothing of the sort.

The nine knights went straight to the palace of the Christian king of Jerusalem, which was situated on the sacred mound, close to where Solomon's Temple had once stood. There they were admitted to the presence of King Baudoin II, who had received the crown of Jerusalem only months before. Baudoin was not of Champagne stock, but he had strong Burgundian connections and must surely have been expecting these particular visitors. He garrisoned them in a large block of stables close to his palace, a place that was right above the old temple. There they remained for nine long years, never seeking recruits, save one; their actions were invisible to history and their true motives for being in Jerusalem are a mystery to this day.

There has been much speculation as to what this strange little band was doing during its protracted stay in Jerusalem. Knight and Lomas in their book *The Hiram Key*[1] suggest that an early Masonic ritual explains exactly what they were up to – they were digging under the floor of the stables, down into the subterranean vaults of the old temple.

> In pursuance of your orders, we repaired to the secret vault, and let down one of the companions as before. The sun at this time was at its meridian height, the rays of which enabled him to discover a small box, or chest, standing on a pedestal, curiously wrought, and overlaid with gold: he gave

---

1 Christopher Knight and Robert Lomas, The Hiram Key, Century, London, 1996.

the signal of ascending, and was immediately drawn out. We have brought the ark up, for the examination of the grand council.

This section of the ritual suggests that among the treasures found by the knights was the famed "Ark of the Covenant." The ark was a wooden box, overlaid with gold and which dated back to before the children of Israel had first entered Palestine. It had supposedly been made on the instructions of God to carry the sacred laws of the people, as laid down to Moses on Mount Sinai.

Whether or not this is actually what the knights found can only be speculation because if the ark was discovered and brought back to Europe, it has never surfaced since. A much more likely scenario is that the object of the search was not so much tangible treasure but rather documents. Among the scrolls found at Qumran in the Jordan Valley back in the 1940s was one made of beaten copper. This was certainly of Essene origin and it gives detailed accounts of where treasure and further documents had been hidden – most likely in face of the imminent threat from the Roman legions. The copper scroll indicates that a large stash was located in subterranean vaults beneath the Temple Mound in Jerusalem.

Of course, the copper scroll from Qumran was not discovered until eight hundred years after the excavations of the knights in Jerusalem but we have seen that there were probably dynastic connections between the Essene and the ruling elite of Champagne. These are emphasized by the similarities in dress, custom, and purpose of the Essene brotherhood and the Cistercians. It isn't beyond the realms of possibility that oral traditions, or perhaps other documentary proof of the location of the Jerusalem hoard, existed in Troyes. By far the most likely scenario is that the rulers of Champagne were well aware of their Jewish Essene heritage and that they were simply attempting to retrieve what their ancestors had carefully hidden immediately prior to the Jewish uprising of AD 70.

Indeed, the finding of the Qumran scrolls and the light this throws upon the Essene and their beliefs makes absolute sense of the Cistercians and the mysterious nine knights, who would, in time, become the famed Knights Templar. The Essene had specifically planned, in minute detail, to create a large army, as part of its own intentions to build a New Jerusalem. As this army would have been to the Essene, so the Knights Templar would become to the Cistercians and their rulers in Troyes.

Perhaps, at some time in the future, the finds of those first Templar knights will come to light, though it is equally likely that they no longer exist. Either way, there is little doubt that the Essene and those who were ruling in Champagne at the start of the twelfth century had a commonness of purpose that cannot be viewed as a coincidence.

It was during their stay in Jerusalem that the nine knights admitted one new member to their band. This was none other than Hugh, Count of Champagne. In 1125 he gave up his titles and traveled to the Holy City, there to become the vassal of Hugh de Payen, reversing the role that had formerly existed between them. His role as Count of Champagne fell to his nephew, who became Thibaud II, Immediately, Thibaud began a series of actions that were demonstrably part of the overall plans that were being carefully hatched. Champagne already had a series of fairs, held at different times of the year in its cities and towns. Thibaud elevated these from being local markets to international trade fairs. He made provision for merchants to store their goods and to be accommodated, at the same time securing safety of passage from neighboring States. Spending lavishly, Thibaud did everything in his power to make certain that the Champagne Fairs would become the most famous and successful gatherings of their kind. In the fullness of time they would attract merchants from all parts of the known world and make Champagne fabulously rich.

We can see with hindsight why the original nine knights, eventually ten in number, had been content to while away their time in Jerusalem. Circumstances back in Champagne had to be right before they could stand a chance of putting the next stage of their plans into action. This was down to Bernard of Clairvaux, who during this period had been steadily building up his influence with the Church authorities, and specifically with the Pope.

By 1128 the time was deemed right and the knights returned to France. By this time Bernard had prevailed upon the Pope, Honorius II, to convene a Council in Troyes. There was plenty of business on the agenda but the item that interested Bernard was his plan to create a new order of fighting monks. This would be named "The Poor Knights of Christ and the Temple of Solomon." The idea must have seemed attractive to the Pope because it has been suggested that this new army would be subject to no authority save that of the Pope himself. At a time when the papacy could be precarious and when papal lands were often under attack, an armed fighting force specifically dedicated to the pontiff must have seemed reassuring to Honorius.

So it was that at the Council of Troyes the new Order was sanctioned and its rule of conduct was created by Bernard himself. The Knights Templar, as they would come to be known, were to be companions and brothers to the Cistercians, though their remit was very different. On paper their purpose was to fight alongside the Crusaders in Palestine. They would be funded by monastic houses created throughout France and beyond, establishing farms that would raise money to send knights and their retinues to the Levant.

Within a very short time Hugh de Payen, the first Grand Master of the Templars, was on the road again, this time traveling to Britain. Others of the original knights went to the South of France. Everywhere they traveled the Templars received a rapturous welcome. Grants of land and money came flooding in. Farms, villages, and eventually towns became Templar property and they lost no time in copying the methods of the Cistercians – turning marginal, unproductive land into havens of fertile prosperity.

At a speed that must have seemed positively meteoric at the time the Templars soon created themselves a formidable fleet of merchant and fighting ships. These were needed to get soldiers and supplies in place but the ships represented the first mercantile venture too. The Templars began by transporting pilgrims to the Holy Land – at a price – but they were soon acting in the capacity of merchants in their own right, trans-shipping produce back and forth from the East and plying the Mediterranean on a daily basis. Before long they became involved in banking, which because of the peculiarity of their position in society, was an avenue they could travel with impunity. At the time it was against Church law for any Christian to charge another Christian interest. The Templars got round this problem in a number of different ways and in any case they were soon so powerful that nobody argued with them.

The Tempars invented credit transactions and provided a means by which merchants could travel the roads and seas of Europe without having to carry vast sums of money with them. Any merchant could deposit a sum of money in one Templar establishment, for example in London. There he would receive a ciphered note that he could pass to another Templar headquarters, say in Troyes, and receive his money in local currency – less interest, of course.

Templar society was not unlike that of the Cistercians and differed only because of the peculiar needs of the institution. Most of the fighting Templars were ordained monks and were attended by sergeants at arms together with those of lower rank. However, the vast majority of Templar personnel never saw the Holy Land. They were farmers, blacksmiths, sailors, butchers, bakers – in fact, engaging in any and every task that would serve to make the Templars richer and more powerful.

As the influence of Bernard of Clairvaux became ever stronger, so the Templars also gained. The next Pope after Honorius II was Innocent II. This man owed his very position as Pope to Bernard, who prevailed upon him to confer ever more rights and privileges upon the Templars. They paid no taxes to the rulers of the countries in which they had lands, they could travel where they pleased with impunity, and eventually they became so powerful that they actually held the treasuries of both France and England along with their own funds. The Templars collected taxes for monarchs and other agencies, making sure of course that they got the necessary cut. They patrolled the roads of Europe, creating turnpikes and building newer and better routes for merchants – paying particular attention to the needs of the rising Champagne Fairs.

Nobody has the remotest idea just how wealthy the Knights Templar actually became because they were ferociously secret and no agency had the right to review their book keeping or to enter any of their establishments. In terms of their religious commitment they shared the virtual obsession of the Cistercians for the Virgin Mary. It was the Virgin's name the Templars cried as they went into battle and Templar graves, especially in the Levant, often depicted the roses of Mary entwined around a Templar sword. What actually went on behind the closed doors of the Templar presbyteries, which were located across the whole of Western Europe and the Near East, will never be known. Like the Cistercians, they were great builders, and in fact far surpassed their monastic cousins in terms of their constructions of castles, churches, and even cathedrals.

The Templars became something of an anachronism. In their later days they were often accused of being high-handed, arrogant, and even bullying, yet it is clear that their intentions were quite different from those of the monarchs in whose countries they lived. One of the most important pieces of legislation ever penned in a European context was a document called Magna Carta. This most certainly represented the first "bill of rights" ever created in Europe. It was signed by the then King of England, John, in June 1215 under pressure from the barons and it specifically laid the foundations for rule by parliament. At the time of the signing of Magna Carta, King John was a "guest" of the Templars in London and the Grand Master of the Templars in England stood at John's right hand as he signed the document. There is little doubt that the Templars sided with the barons in their dispute with John and Magna Carta was the result.

This may also be the first occasion on which we see the Templars at odds with the Catholic Church and in particular the Pope. Innocent III, who occupied the Vatican at the time, had his own reasons for not wanting a document such as Magna Carta to be created or signed in England and in taking part in its composition and signing the Templars were clearly defying the one man who was supposed to be their master.

It is said that the Templars were responsible for a new building technique that began to take Europe by storm in the twelfth century. Gothic architecture differed radically from the Romanesque style that preceded it. Romanesque buildings relied on massive, thick walls to support their rounded arches, whereas in Gothic architecture the use of the pointed arch allowed for a revolution in building techniques. The Gothic arch, more properly known as the "ogive" was much stronger than its rounded cousin and could be used not only in doorways and windows but also combined to create the actual body of a building. Huge vaults became the norm, causing cathedrals and churches to soar to unheard of heights. Stresses within much thinner walls were carried to flying buttresses outside the buildings themselves. Windows became massive and the cathedrals were a blaze of light thanks to their ornate stained glass. As we shall see when we come to look closely at the "pentacle," a geometric figure of great importance to both the Templars and later to Freemasons, there was something very special about the Gothic arch, probably a remnant of the Kabbalistic knowledge the Templars clearly possessed.

The Kabbalah is a body of mystical teachings of ultimately Jewish origin. It probably originated as early as the first century AD. At the heart of the Kabbalah is the belief that there are divine mysteries within the Torah, a sacred Jewish book containing the laws as passed to Moses. During the twelfth century the Kabbalah came to be of significant interest to Christian scholars, particularly in France. Centers of study of the Kabbalah existed in a number of French cities and there was certainly one in Troyes. The Knights Templar continued their association with the Levant for nearly two centuries, where they were mixing with many Jewish and Islamic scholars. It would be extraordinary if they had not interested themselves in the practical application of the Mystery Schools of Judaism and Islam. Some commentators assert that Bernard of Clairvaux had Kabbalistic experts in his own abbey at Clairvaux and since he was clearly steeped in mysticism, this is not at all unlikely.

It is also asserted that the Knights Templar were responsible for the building of the new cathedral of Chartres that was begun in 1194. This was probably the first entirely Gothic cathedral, though the style had first been used back in the days of Bernard of Clairvaux. Bernard's own preferred building style was simple and unadorned, but demonstrates a harmony that he equated with God Himself. Between them the Cistercians and the Templars revolutionized architecture in Europe and there are reasons to believe that there are messages within Gothic architecture that betray some of the true beliefs of both institutions. Their virtual obsession with building and with the mysteries that attended it were passed to the stonemasons' guilds they helped to create and much of the amassed wisdom and the attendant rituals that developed within it passed eventually to Freemasonry.

Despite their phenomenal success and their careful planning, there were eventualities that neither the Cistercians nor the Templars could foresee. One of these came along in the 1280s, a long time after the death of Bernard of Clairvaux but during the period when the Cistercians and especially the Templars were at their zenith.

The whole of Western Europe suffered a series of extremely wet summers and colder than average winters. One of the results was repeated infestations of "sheep scab" a terrible disease that decimated the flocks of both Orders. For the Cistercians it was little short of a disaster. The abbeys, particularly the very large ones in the North of England, had mortgaged their wool crop for years ahead. Wool had to be bought in at massive prices in order to satisfy the contracts and many of the abbeys were on the point of financial ruin. This made them particularly vulnerable to the Crown authorities, especially in England and Scotland. At the same time the Cistercian lay brotherhood was proving to be troublesome and in many locations it was abandoned and less productive granges were sold. The whole infrastructure of the Cistercian Order began to gradually unravel and although in staggered on in England until the Reformation of the sixteenth century, it became a shadow of its former self.

The Templars also suffered in the 1280s because of the sheep scab, but this would not have hit them as hard as the Cistercians because they had so many other resources to fall back on. The real problem for the Templars at around this time was the loss of Jerusalem. This had taken place on 2 October 1187, when the city surrendered to the Islamic forces of Saladin. The Templars weathered this storm because there was still a large Christian presence in the Levant. The final defeat in the Levant came a century later with the fall of Acre in 1291, at which time the Christian armed presence in the Holy Land was finally snuffed out. Neither of these events was the fault of the Templars, who continued to fight with significant bravery to the very end. In reality the defeats were as a result of the lack of will on the part of European monarchs to spend enough to retain the Holy Land. Nevertheless, the Templars came in for significant criticism and were, to a great extent, the scapegoats of the moment.

Those who ordered events in Champagne had little time to think up any new sort of strategy to retain their influence and to keep the momentum of their actions going. Champagne, the very heartland of their power, was itself under threat and had been since 1284. The region had passed by marriage to the kings of Navarre some years earlier but this family seems to have had good relations with the Templars. The problem came when Henry III of Navarre died in 1274, leaving a daughter, Jean of Navarre, to inherit his extensive lands. Jean and her mother fell under the protection, if such a word can be used under the circumstances, of the French crown. The result was that in 1284 Jean of Navarre was married to Philip, who would ascend the throne as King Philip IV of France in the following year. Philip could not immediately take control of Champagne, because it belonged to his wife. However, it effectively came into his possession in 1305 when Jean died and Champagne came to his son Louis. Since Louis was only a child, Philip could justifiably run the Duchy on his behalf.

There was no love lost between Philip IV and the Templars. On more than one occasion they had saved him from angry mobs in Paris and he had, for some time, been lodged in their headquarters in Paris. He knew how wealthy they were and looked on their lands and money avariciously. Philip was also worried about the loss of the Holy Land and the repercussions this might have in Europe. The Templars were massively powerful and controlled a huge army. Rumor had it that they were looking for a kingdom to call their own and the most likely region would be the South of France. Philip did not control this region but he would not have wanted the Templars as neighbors. In addition, he owed them half his kingdom as surety for massive loans. When events are looked at in their context it becomes obvious that Philip had been planning the downfall of the Templars for some time. However, he could not achieve this on his own. The Templars were still under the direct protection of the Pope, so Philip decided to become a Pope-maker in his own right.

It is probable that Philip was complicit in the murder of two Popes, Boniface VIII, who held the Vatican from 1294 until 1303, and then Benedict XII, who lasted a single year from 1303 until 1304. This was because Philip wanted his own man on the papal throne. He achieved his objective in 1304 with the election of Bertrand de Got, a close friend of his from childhood. The French king managed to secure a large number of cardinals to his cause, many of whom were French. With their aid Bertrand became Pope Clement V.

Clement was prevailed upon to quit his residence in Rome and to run the papacy from Avignon in France and together the two friends masterminded the end of the Knights Templar. On Friday 13 October 1307, secret orders went out to storm every Templar property throughout France and to arrest anyone found in them. The charges brought against the Templars were designed to show them to be heretics of the most profound sort. It was said, among other things, that they had sacrificed children, spat upon the cross, and that they had worshiped a mysterious bearded face named Baphomet. They were further accused of having secret links with Islam and performing rites that were not sanctioned by the Church.

Philip IV may have had the satisfaction of gaining much of the land that had formerly been under Templar control, but he received very little else. The huge Templar fleet, normally moored at La Rochelle, mysteriously slipped its moorings on the night of October 12 1307 and disappeared. Virtually no gold was found in Templar properties, even the Commanderies of Paris and Troyes, and the number of Templar personnel arrested was much lower than might have been expected.

It is inconceivable that the Templars had been taken by surprise in 1307. They knew the political situation in France and Champagne as well as anyone and doubtless had spies everywhere. They had almost certainly been taking actions against Philip's move for some time. Stephen Dafoe and I demonstrated in our book, *The Warriors and the Bankers*,[2] that the Templars did indeed create their own kingdom but it wasn't in the South of France. It lay in the high Alps to the South and East of France and would become the country we now know as Switzerland. We were, and remain, astounded that nobody has realized this before. Switzerland is the center of world banking and remains the most secretive nation in the world. It has any number of Templar credentials and was being created from a collection of disparate mountain communities at "exactly" the same time the Templars were being persecuted in France and beyond.

Even aside from Switzerland, the Templars were never totally destroyed. Although the Pope issued a Bull excommunicating the Templars and dissolving them as a Church institution, in many places, for example in Portugal, they simply changed their name and carried on exactly as before. But one fact was not in doubt. The Catholic Church, and in particular the Popes of the Church, had made themselves a powerful enemy – a fact that would not be forgotten in the fullness of time. The revenge of the Templars would be played out by other agencies – those that replaced Templarism. None of these agencies would ever grow more powerful or influential than Freemasonry.

---

2 Alan Butler and Stephen Dafoe, The Warriors and the Bankers, Templar Books, Ontario, 1998.

CHAPTER NINE

FROM TEMPLARISM
TO FREEMASONRY

FROM TEMPLARISM TO FREEMASONRY

Before showing how the Knights Templar survived and passed their peculiar religious, political, and economic beliefs on to other organizations, such as the Freemasons, we need to pause for a moment and look at the legacy of the Templars themselves.

The Grand Master of the Templars, Jacques de Molay, was executed in Paris in 1315, having retracted the confession that had been dragged from him by torture in 1307. By this time Templarism was officially banned in all countries that fell under the sway of the Roman Catholic Church. This policy was fine in principle but it could never work in practice. There were some places, for example in Portugal, where the Templars were so deeply enmeshed in society that to destroy them lock, stock, and barrel would have meant ruin for the very nation. After the initial Templar arrests in 1307, Dinas, the King of Portugal, began a two-year investigation into the accusations against the Templars and ultimately found them to be innocent. Rome was not happy and provided further Bulls insisting that all Templar lands and property should be passed to another, less contentious, military Order, the Knights Hospitaller.

Dinas refused and hedged his bets until a new Pope, John XXII, relented and created a new Order of Knights to replace the Templars in Portugal. These were named "The Knights of Christ" and most of the Portuguese who had been Knights Templar simply became Knights of Christ. Strangely enough the rule followed by the Knights of Christ was that of the Cistercians. In almost every respect they were simply Templars with a slightly different name.

Even though the heartland of French Templarism now lay in the Alps, where Switzerland was gradually coming into existence, the new Knights of Christ began to spread from Portugal into Spain, then Italy and France. In Germany the Teutonic Knights, another offshoot of the Templars, simply refused to disband and nobody was powerful enough to argue the point. Although it cannot be denied that the influence of the Templars as a cohesive force was much reduced in the years after 1307 the clock of history could not be turned back, no matter how much the Church and the monarchs of Europe might have wished it to be. The Cistercians and the Templars between them had altered Europe forever.

Nature and society alike abhor a vacuum. International trade was so well established by 1307 that it certainly was not going to disappear. True, the Champagne Fairs quite quickly went into decline but there were emerging agencies, particularly in Italy, that were ready and willing to fill the void. It was a series of Northern Italian banking families that took over much of the business of the Templars. Their power and influence would eventually lead to the Renaissance – an explosion of scientific and artistic endeavor, funded by rationalism and logic. In turn, the Renaissance would further erode the influence of the Church and set the seal on feudalism. These same Italian banking families contributed to the rise of Florence, and created the first genuine European experiment in democracy since that of the Ancient Greeks.

Meanwhile, it was most certainly in Scotland, a country that never seriously followed the orders of the Vatican to destroy Templarism, that the ideas and influence of the Order eventually passed into Freemasonry. It is suggested by some historians that the missing Templar fleet sailed to Western Scotland in 1307 and though there is no independent proof of this fact, there are strong rumors that Templar Knights fought for Scotland against her old adversary England at Bannockburn in 1314. Robert the Bruce was King of Scotland at the time and was an enthusiastic supporter of the Templars. In fact it is almost certain that he was a Templar himself. It was his earnest wish that, upon his death, his heart should be buried in Jerusalem. He died in 1329 but unfortunately those escorting his remains were attacked in Spain and Bruce's heart eventually found its way back to Scotland. It was buried in a lead container in Melrose Abbey. This is very telling because Melrose was a Cistercian abbey – probably as close to the "New Jerusalem" as Scotland could afford at the time.

Before I demonstrate how Templarism specifically turned itself into Freemasonry there is another avenue that requires attention. For this information I have to thank a colleague and friend, the Scottish historian John Ritchie. John happened to notice that several locations in Scotland that were of specific relevance to the country's history are abbeys built by a little-known monastic Order called the Tironians. The Order was started by Bernard of Thiron. Thiron is now a village in Picardy, France, but Bernard originally came from Abbeville, which is in Normandy.

Bernard of Thiron was born in around 1046 and lived until 1117, which makes him a contemporary of Bernard of Clairvaux. Bernard of Thiron was a reformed Benedictine, who found the Order to be both lax and corrupt. After a considerable period as a hermit, he became the head of an abbey in Thiron, from where he derived the name by which he is most commonly known. Like the Cistercians, the Tironians believed in unremitting toil as a way to greater sanctity.

The Order was especially associated with stonemasonry and in addition to building its own abbeys it completed many churches.

The real importance of the Tironians does not lie in France, but rather in Scotland. They were asked to go there in 1113 to found an abbey at Selkirk. It is likely that the Tironians were invited to Scotland by Queen Margaret (now also St Margaret). She was the mother of one of Scotland's most famous monarchs, David I. In 1128 the Tironians moved to Kelso. This was four years after David had taken the throne and, since he had moved his capital to Roxburgh, he may well have asked for the move, so that the new abbey would be close to his palace there.

St Thiron himself was not always on good terms with other abbeys in France. He had a memorable falling out with the great Benedictine house of Cluny and his eventual foundation was odd in a number of ways. The Tironians maintained a sort of tonsure (haircut) that was not normal at the time. Rather, it harped back to that worn by the Culdean Monks of Celtic Ireland, Scotland, and parts of Northern Anglo-Saxon England. Supposedly this form of tonsure was prohibited after a great Church meeting or synod that took place in Whitby, Yorkshire, England in AD 664. The Tironians were very like Culdeans in other ways. They revered nature and also showed the greatest reverence for the Virgin Mary. Interestingly enough, when the abbey was moved from Selkirk to Kelso it was named "The Abbey of St Mary and St John." St John the Baptist was particularly important to the Knights Templar and is also very significant in Freemasonry.

In addition to founding Selkirk and Kelso, the Tironians were associated with the abbey church at Scone, where the Kings of Scotland were crowned. They also created the abbey at Kilwinning, where there had formerly been a great Culdean church, supposedly founded by St Columba himself.

Catholic historians, and in particular the *Catholic Encyclopaedia*, remain almost silent about the Tironians. Could this be because they showed themselves to be so different to mainstream Roman Catholic monks of their day? The situation is further confused because the Tironians did not keep ordered historical records. What is a fact is that the Tironians were tremendous builders and that they created some of the most magnificent early stone churches and abbeys in Scotland. Nor does anyone doubt that they were, or at any rate became, very Culdean in nature or that they regularly chose to settle in places in Scotland where the Culdees had founded houses centuries before. The Tironians cannot be ruled out as having contributed to the eventual rise of Freemasonry in Scotland, though it is more likely that the Craft came into existence in the village of Rosslyn, close to Edinburgh, as a direct offshoot of the banned Templar Order.

It is most likely that the origins of Freemasonry can be found in the actions of one particular man. His name was William Sinclair, and he was from an old Norman family with impeccable Knights Templar credentials. The Sinclairs had originally been called St Clair. They came from St Clair sur Ept and had fought with distinction alongside William of Normandy at Hastings in 1066. Somehow, in the following years, they acquired land in Scotland and gradually became one of the most powerful families there. Ultimately, following judicious marriages with Scandinavian families, the Sinclairs became princes and then earls of Orkney.

The first Templar establishment on British soil had been on St Clair land. Hugh de Payen, the first Grand Master of the Templars, was married to a St Clair heiress and it was upon land granted by her that the Templars first came after the Council of Troyes. Actually, there is some circumstantial evidence that the land, not far from Edinburgh and in a village that is to this day called "Temple," was actually granted even before the Templars had been sanctioned as an official monastic institution.

In was in the year 1440, over a century after the attacks made on the Templars by the French king, Philip IV, that William Sinclair, the third Prince of Orkney, laid the foundation stone for a unique little church on land just south of Edinburgh. To all intents and purposes Rosslyn Chapel, as the building came to be called, was intended to be the collegiate Church of St Matthew. The building that is still be to be seen on the site, small though it is, has become one of the wonders of Scotland and has attracted so many legends that it is virtually besieged by visitors from all over the world at all times of the year.

Rosslyn Chapel took forty years to complete, despite the fact that the building as we see it today was supposedly only intended to be the "Lady Chapel" of a much larger building. In reality some leading architects have asserted that although the building "looks" as though it is incomplete, in reality it was never intended to be any larger than it is.

What makes Rosslyn almost unique in not only Scottish but British church building is the number of sculptures it contains. Both inside and out Rosslyn is a veritable storybook in stone. Rising from an ornate pillar, close to where the altar now stands, lavish carvings of various plants and flowers spread their tendrils around the whole building. Almost every square inch of the building carries carvings of one sort or another and there are literally dozens of examples of the "Green Man," a figure found in many British churches but never in such great numbers as at Rosslyn.

Strange representations of men hanged by their feet, musicians, knights on horseback, horned kings, and depictions of peasant life join the frenzy of frozen activity throughout the whole rectangular building. Above, dozens of five-pointed stars carved onto the vaulted ceiling, together with a sun and a moon, make this one of the most extraordinary buildings imaginable.

There can be no doubt that the rich symbolism written into the stone of Rosslyn is meant to signify something important but a great percentage of it looks distinctly un-Christian. The Green Man is a good example.

An example of the Green Man

Although the Green Man is to be found in many British churches, he is usually seen in ones or twos. Almost never is he to be found in every corner of a building and it is usual to find him hidden away under the seats in the choir, known as misericords. In Rosslyn Chapel the Green Man is the rule rather than the exception and, as John

Ritchie has pointed out, his face ages around the building. On the East wall he appears young and vibrant, while on the South wall the foliage is more luxuriant and the faces older looking. On the West wall the Green Man is definitely aging, and finally on the North wall we find fewer Green Men but many carved skulls.

Few doubt that the Green Man, who can also be found in locations as far away as India, represents the face of nature. However, in Rosslyn Chapel it seems certain that he depicts the seasonal qualities of nature and that he is representative of annually dying and reborn vegetation, or the corn god mentioned earlier.

One of the real puzzles of the Rosslyn Chapel carvings is that some of them depict plant species, such as aloes and maize, that were supposedly unknown in Britain when the chapel was built. It has been suggested that this represents proof positive that the Sinclairs, who were great sailors with a partly Viking ancestry, had visited the New World, decades ahead of Columbus. In fact, there are stories about such a journey and it is now accepted by many that the Knights Templar had been regular visitors to the shores of North America.

Below Rosslyn is a crypt. Here, according to Sinclair family tradition, are to be found past members of the family, laid to rest in their armor. They may, in fact, be guarding something of great worth and of historical antiquity. As far as I am aware it was the authors Christopher Knight and Robert Lomas who first suggested that Rosslyn Chapel is a deliberate copy of the Temple of Solomon that once stood in Jerusalem. This might not be as farfetched as it first appears. Nobody with a feel for British churches could be left in any doubt that Rosslyn Chapel stands out like a sore thumb. I have personally visited hundreds, if not thousands of churches across Britain and I have never encountered one that seemed less church-like. In form the building definitely is more of a temple and the altar at the East end seems like an interloper or an afterthought.

Tradition has it that while Rosslyn Chapel was being constructed, William Sinclair's house caught fire. He was panic-stricken regarding the fate of a number of large wooden boxes, which he insisted were rescued before anything else. These boxes, it is suggested, contained "something" that eventually found its way into a sealed chamber far below even the crypt of the chapel. What they contained is not known and those responsible for Rosslyn Chapel seem very reluctant to allow any form of invasive archaeology to take place below the floor of the building. Every conceivable suggestion has been made for the supposed treasure of Rosslyn Chapel, even to the possibility of the head of Jesus himself having been buried there.

The most likely explanation from my perspective is that the wooden crates contained the documents and perhaps other items recovered by the Knights Templar from the real Temple of Solomon, back in the twelfth century. These could easily have been brought out of France in the months leading up to the attack made on the Templars in 1307. They could even have been aboard the ships that disappeared from La Rochelle on 12 October 1307.

Rosslyn Chapel, small though it is, took 40 years to complete. It represents the combined skills of dozens of stonemasons and stone carvers. Undoubtedly it is a deliberate picture book in stone and William Sinclair had to trust those who created his masterpiece to keep the secrets it contains. If there is any treasure locked away in a subterranean vault, those who worked on the chapel must have been aware of the fact. At the time the chapel was built the Catholic Church was still deeply suspicious of anything to do with the Knights Templar, and doubtless fearful of retribution for the action it had taken against them. It would therefore have been most unwise for the Sinclair family to allow any hint of the secrets the building contained to become common knowledge. But how could William Sinclair make absolutely certain that his workers would carry what they knew to their graves?

The answer seems to be that he employed something that naturally existed amongst stonemasons at the time – their natural tendency to be secretive about their work and their strong commitment to the stonemasons' guild of which they were a part. William Sinclair shared some of the most guarded secrets of Templarism with his workers, deepening the affiliation they had to their guild and, by way of horrible oaths, ensuring their continued and willing silence.

This, it is suggested, is the way Freemasonry came into existence and it seems to me to be the most likely explanation. With the passing of time there was a strong desire among gentlemen in the district to be made party to this "secret society" even though they were not stonemasons themselves. As a result "speculative Freemasonry" came into existence, which carried the traditions, stories, and rituals created by William Sinclair but which did not require that those taking part were themselves craftsmen.

It is known that in 1491 stonemasons in Edinburgh were granted the right "to gett a recreation in the common lodge," an inference that they were doing something other than simply talking about their trade. By 1599 we find the first veiled reference to the existence of a lodge that was something other than a trade organization. It was in this year that William Schaw, Master of Work and Warden General for King James VI, made reference to Lodge 0, which was at Killwinning. This was referred to as the "Mother Lodge" of Scotland and seems already to have been a speculative rather than an operative lodge. Killwinning was a location that had been famous on account of the abbey built there by the ever industrious

Tironian monks, who themselves had been building on foundations that went back to the Culdees and Columba himself.

Other lodges quickly followed and, as we have seen, Freemasonry probably came South of the border when James IV of Scotland became James I of England in 1603, though there are some slight indications that it may already have existed in London.

Thus we find in Freemasonry a heady fusion of post-Templar beliefs and practices, suffused with elements of the Culdean heritage. It retained the strong element of worship for the Virgin Mary that had permeated the Cistercians, the Tironians, and the Templars but also had a deep element of nature worship. This emanated not only from native British history but also from the Mystery religions from much further away.

The specific reverence for the Virgin Mary that permeated Freemasonry at its commencement, and which can still be recognized today, was not at odds with what was taking place within the Catholic Church at the time – it had been present for many hundreds of years. In fact, the cult of the Virgin had been present in Catholicism virtually from its inception. The Vatican constantly fought against what was much more than an irritant and which at times took on the form of a "schism." It was still fighting in the nineteenth century. This might seem strange. After all, what did the Church have to fear from the Virgin Mary, one of its most prominent icons? In order to understand this we have to see how powerful the cult of the Virgin actually was and how far back in time it went.

CHAPTER TEN

THE CULT OF MARY

THE CULT OF MARY

Malta is a small group of islands in the Mediterranean Sea. On the two major and one minor island that make up present-day Malta, there are some 365 Catholic churches, which is a staggering number considering the size of Malta and its relatively small population. I visited Malta on a research trip two years ago and I was staggered, not only by the physical number of churches in this small space, but also by the form of worship that takes place there. Of course, it wasn't possible for me to visit every church, but I did take in a broad cross section. All of these buildings contain the usual symbols one would expect in an average Catholic church, though the number of depictions of the Virgin Mary in her guise as "Queen of Heaven" is staggering, with life-sized or larger-than-life statues present in almost every case. These are beautifully made and sumptuously adorned. There are cases of churches in Malta where almost no iconography relating to Jesus or God is present but in which Mary is represented time and again.

This fact may be something of an embarrassment to the Church authorities in Malta because on more than one occasion it was pointed out to me by official guides that the Maltese definitely "do not" worship Mary, but treat her only as a conduit for approaching the Godhead. Whether or not this is understood or accepted by the majority of Maltese church worshipers is open to question. Malta may be something of an exception bearing in mind the intensity of Mary worship that is openly displayed there, but it remains a good example of what the cult of the Virgin Mary became in Western Europe and beyond.

The Catholic Church has, over the centuries, taken a series of steps to ensure that the position of Mary within its worship cannot be doubted, at least on paper, and we shall deal with these in due course. But it remains a fact that any alien who visited our world for the first time and who had cause to visit a succession of Catholic churches, must undoubtedly reach the conclusion that here was a religion dedicated almost solely to an all-powerful goddess and her murdered son.

One might ask the question "How did this state of affairs come about in the first place?" After all, the Virgin Mary actually plays quite a minor role in the official and accepted Christian gospels. In New Testament terms her position is, at best, passive and she speaks directly only three times. On one of these occasions, in

Luke 1:46-55 we find her quoting what became known as "The Magnificat." In what is her only major speech in the whole New Testament she responds to the fact that God has singled her out to bear his son, Jesus. She says:

> My soul doth magnify the Lord,
> And my spirit hath rejoiced in God my Saviour.
> For he hath regarded the low estate of his handmaiden:
> for, behold, from henceforth all generations shall call me blessed.
> For he that is mighty hath done to me great things;
> and holy is his name.
> And his mercy is on them that fear him from generation to generation.
> He hath shewed strength with his arm;
> he hath scattered the proud in the imagination of their hearts.
> He hath put down the mighty from their seats,
> He hath filled the hungry with good things;
> and the rich he hath sent empty away.
> He hath helped his servant Israel, in remembrance of his mercy;
> As he spake to our fathers, to Abraham, and to his seed for ever.

Even these may not be Mary's own words. There isn't much doubt that the Magnificat is ultimately of Old Testament origin. Something very similar to it appears in 1 Samuel 2 and is known as "The Song of Hannah."

It is difficult to imagine a more humble response on the part of the Virgin Mary to the great favor that has been bestowed upon her, yet this attitude is well out of kilter with the position she presently holds in the minds and hearts of Catholics all over the world. And it does not address a couple of central problems in theology that have taxed the minds of great thinkers for generations. Although some of its highest authorities might wish to do so, the Catholic Church cannot deny two descriptions of Mary that remain central to its doctrine. Mary is, in the eyes of the Church:

1. The Mother of God, and
2. The Queen of Heaven.

Herein lies a great puzzle. It was decided very early on in the evolution of the Christian Church that Jesus was not simply "the son of God" but that he was indivisible from God – in other words he is the "same thing" as God – He is God.

This being the case, if Mary is the Mother of Jesus and Jesus is God, then quite obviously Mary has the right to be called the Mother of God. In a chicken and egg situation carried to the level of absurdity there is a natural implication that if Mary is the Mother of God, she must predate God. In any case, who but a deity could give birth to a deity?

The logical pursuit of these two titles, Mother of God and Queen of Heaven, leads to an even stranger realization. If Jesus is God, and Mary is the Mother of Jesus, she must also be the Bride of God, but with Mary reduced to nothing but the rank of a handmaiden, none of this makes the remotest sense. However, in terms of ancient religions, such as that of the Minoans of Crete for example, there was no problem at all. To these people God was "cyclic," in other words he was born, grew, and died annually, whereas his mother and wife, the Goddess, was eternal. It might be assumed that the Virgin Mary has been grafted onto Christianity for some specific reason, retaining many of the attributes of the old Goddess, but being demoted in terms of her divinity. How could such a situation have come about?

To discover the answer we have to go far back to the origins of the Christian Church. To the very earliest Christians the familiar Trinity of Father, Son, and Holy Spirit was almost certainly viewed very differently than it is today. The original name given to the Holy Spirit was "Sophia," a Greek word meaning wisdom. However it is a word loaded with symbolism, primarily because it has a strong feminine connotation. An early representation of the Holy Spirit, and one that is mentioned in the New Testament in connection with Jesus' own baptism in the Jordan, is a dove. The dove is still used regularly in Christian iconography but it is far from being unique to Christianity. All over the ancient world it was a symbol for the Great Goddess. There are examples of model shrines, found in the ruins of the Palace of Knossos in Crete, in which there is no formal representation of the Goddess, but doves surmount the temple columns, indicating her presence. The dove was associated with almost every form of the ancient Goddess, including Isis, Demeter, Ishtar, Iris, and the British goddess Bridget.

The form of the dove and the word Sophia are intimately related and Sophia also had a particular relevance to the Knights Templar. A leading expert on the Old Testament, the late Doctor Hugh Schonfield, discovered to his absolute incredulity that the Templars had used a very ancient form of cipher that was of specific importance to groups such as the Essene. This is called the Atbash Cipher. The Atbash is a word substitution cipher that allows a particular passage of script to have an apparent meaning, but in fact to have a very different meaning to those who are in the know. Schonfield was drawn to the word "Baphomet." Baphomet is supposed to have been some sort of deity worshiped by the Templars and the name was mentioned in 1307 in connection to one of the charges brought against them. When applied to the Atbash Cipher there is no doubt whatsoever what Baphomet actually represents. It is "Sophia."

It is almost certain that to very early Christians, and most likely to the Knights Templar and their cousins the Cistercians too, the Father, Son, and Holy Ghost of the modern Trinity was actually equated to the Young God, the Old God, and the Goddess of ancient tradition. Only with the deeply patriarchal society that was the legacy of the Roman Empire did the Holy Spirit lose its gender association and take on the rather ambiguous position it enjoys today. The fact that the Templars knew and guarded this word demonstrates that its true importance and meaning were never really lost.

Theological problems came and went within the early Church after the Council of Nicea in 325. Then, in 553, the Second Council of Constantinople met, once again to pronounce upon the position of Jesus with regard to the Godhead. However, at this meeting Mary was specifically referred to as "Theotokus" – the God Bearer – and it seems evident that she was already the center of what would eventually amount to a "schism" within the Church.   By this period the prayer known as the Ave Maria was already two hundred years old. It had first appeared in Constantinople only eight years after the Council of Nicea. It is still recited by Catholics all over the world on a daily basis.

Hail Mary, full of Grace
The Lord is with thee.

Probably also by the Second Council of Constantinople the greeting given to Mary by Elizabeth, her cousin, and mentioned in the Gospel of St Luke was added, so the prayer became:

Hail Mary, full of Grace
The Lord is with thee.
Blessed art thou amongst women
And blessed is the fruit of thy womb.

At an unknown date the third part of the Ave Maria or Hail Mary appeared, so that the final prayer is:

Hail Mary, full of Grace
The Lord is with thee.
Blessed art thou amongst women
And blessed is the fruit of thy womb.
Holy Mary, Mother of God
Pray for us sinners now and at the hour of our death.

The special reverence for the Virgin Mary is understandable for many different reasons. Not least among these is the fact that Christianity was "imposed" on many millions of people after the fourth century. These were individuals who knew nothing about either it or its origins. A large proportion of these people lived at a great distance from the center of the empire. They had kept their own religions and traditions from time out of mind. To try and enforce a belief pattern was a new departure for Rome during the days of the Emperor Constantine. One of the great successes of the old empire lay in the fact that Rome had its own rich pantheon, which was not simply local in nature but culled from around the known world. Early Roman emperors did not care at all what beliefs any of their subjects might have, just as long as they maintained their obligations to the empire. In fact, Rome went out of its way to accommodate foreign belief patterns and, where possible, to assimilate them.

Just as surely as we can now see Roman Catholicism in Central and South America taking on a very distinct local flavor, affected as it is by pre-Columbian beliefs, so the new religion was seen differently in the many nations upon which it landed in the fourth century. In Britain, for example, Christianity had already taken root before the withdrawal of the Roman legions in the fifth century. In places, and in particular in Ireland, it withstood the later onslaught of centuries of barbarian attack and infiltration. During this period it developed its own character and one that was deeply tinged by the pre-Christian, druidic beliefs of the British Isles. The same was broadly true in Gaul. When Clovis became the first Christian Frankish King in 496, most of those brought to preach Christianity to his people were from Britain or Ireland. The resultant Church bore little similarity to that in Rome. By the time centralization took place under the Carolingian kings the damage was done and some of the heretical Christian beliefs of Western Europe were too strong to be eradicated.

At the same time old deities, which locals were loath to forget, became attached to the Church as saints. St Bridget is a good example. "Brigga" or "Brig" was probably the most important female deity in Britain prior to the arrival of the

Romans and, as in so many other cases, the population were not willing to abandon her and her sister goddesses. Local Church authorities accepted this state of affairs and it was quite natural that much of the reverence for the old tutelary Goddesses of the West was heaped on the only figure available in the Christian story – the Virgin Mary.

During the rule of the Roman Empire many of the great cities of France had become strong centers of Isis worship. In itself this was probably a response to earlier, local deities that were identified by the Roman authorities with Isis. It has been suggested by the writer Louis Charpentier[1] that many of the cities that were important to the Franks maintained a strong association with Isis. He points out that many of these still retain an affix to their name that demonstrates this connection. He suggests that Troyes was originally Troy-is, and that Rheims was once Rheim-is. Similarly we have Chartres as Chartr-is, whilst Paris retains its original "is" ending. The "is" in this context is part of the sacred name of Isis.

It would have been utterly impossible for the empire, with its new religion, to expect that old beliefs, nurtured across so many thousands of years, would suddenly be abandoned. Instead they were subsumed. This was almost certainly the case with the Franks, many of whom retained a deep reverence for an ancient goddess by the name of Rosemerta. She was still of major importance in Lorraine and parts of Northern France by the time of St Bernard of Clairvaux. In Sion de Vaudemont she had been declared "Queen of Heaven" before Christianity arrived, so it was natural that the similarities between her and the Virgin Mary should be recognized and that the two characters should become entwined.

Another part of the growing power of the Virgin Mary had come from much further East. She was particularly venerated in the Byzantian Empire, which was centered upon Constantinople. This area had been a great region of Goddess devotion since very ancient times and the Virgin simply replaced old deities, such as Artemis, who had been the protector of the city. With the arrival of Christianity Constantinople simply switched its allegiance to the Virgin Mary. The great Church of Hagia Sophia in what is now Istanbul but was once Constantinople is dedicated to her and of course still retains the "Sophia" element that equates the Virgin with the Holy Spirit. Images of the Virgin, so tenderly and masterfully created in the East, found their way to Western Europe and there fuelled the rising cult of the Virgin Mary.

---

1 Louis Charpentier, The Mystery of Chartres Cathedral, Avon, London, 1980.

Most authorities agree that the real point at which the cult of the Virgin Mary took off in Western Europe was during the twelfth century and experts on the subject generally make specific reference to St Bernard of Clairvaux. As in so many ways Bernard recreated the Virgin Mary to suit his own particular needs and those of the agencies he served. He wrote many sermons related to the Song of Songs, an Old Testament book attributed to King Solomon. Actually it is odd that the Song of Songs ever made it into the Bible because it has more in common with the love poetry of figures such as Omar Khayyam. St Bernard doubtless hit upon this strange little book for a couple of reasons. This was partly because of its association with Solomon, for whom he and his compatriots had a particular reverence. Even more to the point is the fact that the Song of Songs details a love story between a bride and a bridegroom, both of whom remain anonymous. St Bernard equated the Bridegroom with Jesus and the Bride with both the Virgin Mary and the Church. It may well have been St Bernard who first referred to Mary as "The Bride of Jesus." Modern Christian authorities suggest that St Bernard was speaking figuratively but the term seems quite unambiguous to me.

Thanks in the main to St Bernard of Clairvaux and the Cistercians, the Virgin Mary moved closer and closer to the center of Catholic worship from the twelfth century on. In fact, all the reformed Benedictine Orders held her in the highest esteem and this might be partly because they either resurrected or had maintained a much earlier Culdean attitude towards faith. If the Church worried about this state of affairs, it never took any specific action and it wasn't really until the nineteenth century that suggestions were made that the status of the Virgin Mary needed to be spelled out in letters so big that Catholics could not ignore them.

It is possible that one of the reasons why "Marionism" as it came to be called was not stamped upon earlier was because the Catholic Church had other things to worry about. By the beginning of the sixteenth century the Vatican was being run like a business and not all of its managing directors were equally capable. Neither did they display either the genuine holiness or integrity necessary for the role of Pope. Matters came to a head in March 1513 when Giovanni de Medici was elected as Pope Leo X.

As a member of the most powerful family in Italy at the time, Leo X was the logical choice from a practical point of view but his lavish lifestyle and profligate ways soon caused problems – he simply ran out of money. Leo cast around for ways to fill his coffers and hit upon the very lucrative sideline of selling indulgences. Very soon, for a modest sum, Catholics across the whole of Europe and beyond could "buy" themselves into heaven. The Pope was the direct representative of God on earth and if he said that a particular person's sins were wiped out, then in Catholic law they were. Leo sent his agents everywhere, collecting money from ordinary Catholics and issuing them with receipts that promised them redemption from their sins. This behavior certainly had the desired effect in terms of the Vatican's wealth but it began to foster ill will and even downright opposition from some members of the Church who were sensible enough to realize that the selling of indulgences was nothing but a scandal.

Leo X didn't realize it at the time but he had single-handedly inspired a split within the Church that would cost hundreds of thousands of lives and which would change the face of Christendom forever. What followed was known as the Reformation and it led to the creation of Protestantism.

There were to be significant differences between Roman Catholicism and Protestantism and these remain with us today. There are many denominations of Protestants but generally speaking they differ from Catholics in the way they approach God. Protestants came to rely more on the Word of God through the Scriptures and less through an agency such as the Pope. They not only disliked the obvious farce of selling indulgences but also turned away from a belief in the intervention of saints, the worship of relics, and many of the trappings of the Catholic Mass. Many Protestants strove for a form of simplicity in worship that actually had much in common with the reformed Benedictine Orders, such as the Cistercians, but which owed little to the pomp, ceremony, and, some said, rank corruption that had become commonplace in Catholicism.

Walking into the average nonconformist Church these days, the interested party will see little that was and remains familiar to Catholics. Iconography, such as statues of Mary or Jesus, is generally frowned upon and there is often nothing more than a simple wooden cross and a plain communion table to indicate that this is a place of worship. Does this mean that the Reformation stopped the cult of the Virgin Mary in its tracks? Definitely not – at least not in the minds of those who were most responsible for this major split in the Christian family.

The man who had the most to do with the beginning of the Reformation was an Augustinian monk from Germany. His name was Martin Luther and he was born in Eisleben in 1483. Luther was an intellectual, but also a devout believer. As both a priest and an educator, Luther gradually became more and more disillusioned about some of the practices of the Catholic Church, and in particular the selling of indulgences. This eventually led him to write the famous 95 Theses, which were criticisms of the Church and its practices. These he nailed to the door of Wittenberg Castle Church and this is generally accepted as the first thrust of the Reformation that was to come.

Luther went on to create a split within the Western Christian Church that would lead to wholesale war and destruction across large areas of Europe, but although he had little time for many of the trappings of Catholicism, he retained a strong personal respect and a reverence for the Virgin Mary. This fact might come as a surprise to those who assume the special position occupied by Mary within the Church came to an end with the arrival of Protestantism.

Luther said of Mary:

The veneration of Mary is inscribed in the very depths of the human heart. (Taken from a sermon given on 1 September 1522)

No woman is like you. You are more than Eve or Sarah, blessed above all nobility, wisdom, and sanctity. (Part of a sermon offered at the Feast of the Visitation, 1537)

Mary is his true Mother … (Taken from a Sermon given at Christmas, 1522)

… she is rightly called not only the mother of the man, but also the Mother of God … it is certain that Mary is the Mother of the real and true God. (Taken from a sermon on John 14:16)

Nor was Martin Luther alone as a major Church reformer in his opinions of Mary. John Calvin (1509–1564), the founder of what eventually came to be one of the most austere forms of Protestantism, also revered the Blessed Virgin. Although many would think Calvin to be the least likely candidate for Marionism, he referred to Mary as: "Mary, ever virgin, mother of God" (from a sermon in 1524). He also insisted:

I have never thought, still less taught, or declared publicly, anything concerning the subject of the ever Virgin Mary, Mother of our salvation, which could be considered dishonorable, impious, unworthy, or evil … I believe with all my heart according to the word of holy gospel that this pure virgin bore for us the Son of God. (From a sermon in 1524)

And the very last pamphlet he created in 1564 was entitled "Fidei expositio." It represented a specific insistence on the perpetual virginity of Mary.

Nevertheless, as the Protestants gained ground and their leaders eventually became as tyrannical as those in Rome sometimes were, the veneration of Mary was driven underground. She still retained a special place in the hearts of Anglicans but to the leaders of the Puritans and other nonconformist denominations she seemed to be a focus of popery and superstition.

Mary remains of supreme importance to Catholics to this day, though now within defined limits. These limits were only set by the Vatican in the nineteenth and twentieth centuries. As we shall see, the Church was responding to a dangerous new cult of Mary that was developing in the eighteenth and nineteenth centuries and which was typified by the Vision of La Salette.

CHAPTER ELEVEN

FREEMASONRY AND THE RISE OF SCIENCE

FREEMASONRY AND THE RISE OF SCIENCE

Documented accounts of formalized Freemasonry in England are hard to find prior to the creation of Grand Lodge in London in 1717. Nevertheless, they do exist. One record in particular is especially important to English Freemasonry. This is an entry in the records of an Edinburgh Freemasonic Lodge during the year 1641. The Lodge, or at least part of it, was away from home. A Scottish army had marched South into England and was garrisoned at Newcastle-upon-Tyne. It was there that the first recorded initiation of a Freemason took place on English soil. The recipient was a man by the name of Robert Moray and his importance to modern science cannot be understated.

Moray was a man of ultimately Highland origin, from a solid Scottish family with a rich heritage. He had been born in 1609, which meant he was about 32 when he took his first steps along the Masonic road. He had joined the Scots Guards as quite a young man and had been with the Guards in France where they had done great service under the direct authority of the French crown. Robert Moray seems to have made a singular impression because he became a firm favorite of the French Minister Cardinal Richelieu. Returning to Britain at the outbreak of the English Civil War, Moray was engaged in negotiations with the errant King Charles I, who was at war with Parliament. After the execution of Charles I, and the eventual restoration of the monarchy, Moray was rewarded by the new king and took up residence in London.

What sets Sir Robert Moray apart, in addition to him being the first recorded Freemason initiated on English soil, was the fact that as well as being an admirable soldier, he was an educated man with an interest in science. His family included those of strong Rosicrucian beliefs. The Rosicrucians were a sect that appeared in the seventeenth century, probably in Germany. Their beliefs were a heady cocktail of gnosticism with a strong accent on the female quality in nature and religion. They had much in common with early Freemasonry but also showed a reverence for alchemy, itself the father of science. Moray was one of the founder members of the "Royal Society," an institution that was virtually synonymous with Freemasonry and which was founded in the year 1660.

The Royal Society arose out of a fairly shadowy group of people who have been christened the "Invisible College." The Invisible College betrays its origins by the place it chose to host the first meeting as the Royal Society, which took place on Wednesday 28 November 1660. Its members gathered, as had many of them from at least 1645, in Gresham College. This location might give us a clue as to the unrecorded past of a much earlier English Freemasonry.

Gresham College had originally been the house of Sir Thomas Gresham, a courtier of Queen Elizabeth I. Sir Thomas Gresham was a spy, a mercer, a financier, and one of the greatest bankers of his age. He is probably best remembered for having set up the Royal Exchange in London in the year 1565. The Royal Exchange was responsible for much of the trade coming to and from Elizabethan England and its creation was an attempt to wrest international trade from Antwerp.

Gresham mixed with many of those at Elizabeth's court, among them two particular characters, Dr John Dee and Sir Walter Raleigh. Dee was a philosopher, magician, alchemist, and proto-scientist. He was an indispensable aid to Queen Elizabeth, who relied on both his scientific acumen and his abilities as an astrologer. Dee was a close associate of Sir Walter Raleigh, at one time a favorite of the queen and another man of culture who delighted in both science and mysticism.

Both Dee and Raleigh are directly associated with the birth of the Roiscrucian movement and neither was much interested in either Catholicism or the Church in England. They were, in their own age, radical free thinkers who were always likely to fall foul of the authorities for their own Renaissance-motivated views. However, they were offered a degree of protection during Elizabeth's reign, partly because they were men of influence and power, but probably also because Elizabeth was, in her heart at least, a fairly radical thinker herself.

These men, if not Freemasons themselves, were certainly forerunners of the Craft. When it came to closet religious beliefs they were in a unique position. Queen Elizabeth I had, for mainly political reasons, chosen never to marry. As a result she became known as the "Virgin Queen." With the loss to the country of the Catholic faith, she quite deliberately took on the persona of the Virgin Mary and helped to fill the yawning gap that had been left by the Reformation. The depth of religious feeling surrounding her was quite staggering and created its own iconography. She was portrayed as "Gloriana" and became a physical manifestation of Britannia, who was to the British what Liberty would mean to the Americans. In essence, she was a living version of the Goddess.

The men who came together in November 1660 at Gresham College were meeting in an establishment that was still unusual for its time. When Sir Thomas Gresham had died in 1579, he had left his house in Bishopsgate, London, together with a large bequest, to become a college. This was not to be an exclusive establishment but rather would offer instruction and lectures to anyone who wished to come along. Gresham's own Masonic standing may be relevant because he was certainly made General Warden of Masons in 1567, a title that probably meant more than simply overseeing building projects. His college still served its purpose by the time of the English Civil War. Lectures there included divinity, medicine, geometry, astronomy, rhetoric, and music. Sir Thomas Gresham's own Masonic connections may have been part of the reason why those who were known as the "Invisible College" chose to meet there, and when King Charles II took his British throne, he was happy to give his royal patronage to the Invisible College, making it the Royal Society.

What is extraordinary about the group that formed the Royal Society is that they comprised two factions that had been, until very recently, implacable enemies. Some of them were Royalists, while others were Parliamentarians, the two sides that had fought the bitter and bloody English Civil War between 1642 and 1649. The period between 1649 and 1660 had seen England under the "Commonwealth" administered in the main by the Lord Protector, Oliver Cromwell.

The factor that allowed these old enemies to join together in a common purpose was almost certainly Freemasonry. Sir Robert Moray, who chaired the first meeting of the Royal Society was already a Freemason, and it is very likely that a number of the other members present were also Brother Masons.

Another founder member of the Royal Society was Elias Ashmole, Ashmole was a saddler, turned chemist and antiquarian who had married a rich wife. He was born around 1617 and he was certainly a Freemason because he mentions Lodge meetings in his own journal.

Only twelve men comprised the meeting in November 1660 but once the Society's rules were laid down – rules that in themselves sound distinctly Masonic – forty members were invited to form the new Royal Society. Many of these were professional scientists and some were "gentlemen" who simply had an interest in science. Another of the founder members of the Society was Sir Christopher Wren, the man who was most responsible for rebuilding London after the Great Fire of 1666. He certainly became a Freemason, probably in 1691, but another Masonic founder member of the Royal Society, John Aubrey, claimed that Wren was already a leading Freemason in 1660.

John Locke, a political theorist, who was to become a prominent member of the Royal Society, was certainly a Freemason by 1669, while the famous scientist Robert Boyle was initiated soon after the founding of the Royal Society. Freemasonic credentials were not essential to being elected to the Royal Society, it was simply a case that many of those interested in the promotion of rational thinking and science were either already Masons, or would become allied to the Craft as a result of association with others. One man who cannot be excluded from the list of slightly later members of the Royal Society was Benjamin Franklin, whose own Masonic credentials are not in doubt.

Meanwhile, across the English Channel in France, the French Academy of Sciences was formed just six years after the Royal Society and served a very similar function – the promotion of rational, scientific study and the discovery of its applications that might aid society. It is difficult to assess whether those who founded the French Academy were already Freemasons. Until the very end of the seventeenth century France was still under royal autocratic rule. Early French Freemasons were generally quite politically motivated and became associated with the unrest that eventually led to the French Revolution. Since the French Academy eventually came under the patronage of the French crown, in 1799, it is possible that members who were already Freemasons kept quiet about the fact, or else did not become Academicians until after the Revolution. There was a close association between the monarchy of France and the Catholic Church. The Church already despised Freemasonry and it had little respect for those of a scientific bent either.

Probably the most influential Freemason whom we can first associate with the French Academy of Science was Charles-Maurice Talleyrand Perigord. Known to history simply as Talleyrand, Charles-Maurice was more a phenomenon than a man. Born in February 1754, Talleyrand was disinherited by his aristocratic family on account of having been born with a clubfoot. As a result he decided to enter the Church. Talleyrand would prove to be a radical, a revolutionary, and a religious freethinker, as well as a Freemason. During his training he proved rather an unlikely priest, indulging in a sordid affair with an actress from the Comédie Française.

Against all the odds Talleyrand eventually gained Holy Orders and, even more incredibly, in 1788, mainly because of the influence of his father, he was made Bishop of Autun. He readily joined the revolutionaries and for a while after the French king's arrest he served in a high office, stripping the Church, that he had previously defended so strenuously, of much of its property. Eventually he fell foul of the changing political scene and had to flee to England and then to America. He returned to France in 1796, no longer under threat, and eventually became a high-ranking minister under the rule of Napoleon Bonaparte.

Like many members of the Academy of Sciences at the time, Talleyrand was instrumental in putting forward the suggestion that a new measuring system was required for both France and for the world. He saw this as being an essential component of the new scientific world that would overthrow the perceived tyranny of both feudalism and the Catholic Church. He regularly traveled to London. There he moved in Masonic circles and among the members of the Royal Society. He did everything within his power to encourage co-operation over the suggested metric system, at the same time trying to avert an almost inevitable clash between Britain and France.

At the time Talleyrand was trying to influence the Royal Society, a commission to look into weights and measures had been set up in France, comprising a sub-committee of the French Academy of Science. Included on this sub-committee were names that would become legends in science, men such as Laplace, Lagrange, Monge, Borda, and Condorcet. These were all prominent members of the French Academy of Science and at least three of them are known to have been Freemasons. There are good indications that the French Academy of Sciences, at least after the French Revolution, was as Masonically based as its British counterpart, the Royal Society.

The Royal Society went from strength to strength. Its efforts might have been curtailed by the crowning of the brother of Charles II, who was an acknowledged Catholic. However, James II was king for a very brief time. As a result of what was known as the Glorious Revolution, a bloodless coup in 1688 that ousted the Catholic James, Britain gained new monarchs in the form of William of Orange and his wife Mary Stewart. The plot to get rid of James had been hatched by a political party known as the "Whigs." Included among their number were a great many Freemasons, while leading members of the Royal Society, for example Sir Isaac Newton, also bravely backed the rebellion. William of Orange, who became King William III was also a Freemason.

After James II had been ousted it was made illegal for a Catholic to ever take the throne of Britain. When William died, his sister-in-law Queen Anne came to the throne and on her death, in 1714, the Protestant German George, Elector of Hanover was invited to become George I.

Freemasonry, which until that point had not taken a prominent role in society – probably partly because of the threat of a Catholic monarch, now reformed itself and took a leading place in the scientific and administrative life of Britain.

Although imbued with elements of the ancient mysteries and replete with ceremonies that display its heretical beliefs, Freemasonry has always had strong scientific leanings. At its core lies a fascination for geometry and astronomy. It is has also been deeply influenced by a strong political motivation for freedom and personal choice. All these qualities made it inevitable that it would fall foul of the established Church. Only a few decades before the founding of the Royal Society in England, scientists such as the Italian Galileo were falling foul of the Vatican. Galileo had dared to suggest that it wasn't the earth but rather the sun that lay at the heart of the solar system. For this assertion he faced the Inquisition. He narrowly escaped with his life and was put under perpetual house arrest.

While the Vatican struggled ferociously to keep scientists in check across Europe, it had no control over those in England. Inevitably, advances in Britain and other Protestant countries found their way back into the Catholic heartland and there they further eroded the power and influence of the Church. At the heart of these scientific advances, successive Popes recognized the influence of Freemasonry and they were furious that they could do nothing to alter the situation. The first official reaction to Freemasonry from the Vatican came in 1736, when Pope Clement XII condemned the Craft in the first of twenty papal Bulls that were to follow.

It was and remains the explicit conviction of the Vatican that Freemasonry has a specific agenda – the deliberate and absolute destruction of the Roman Catholic Church. The advances in science brought about in the main by those of Masonic persuasion have been part of the problem. Science is rational. It has no bias and is based on "evidence" rather than "faith." In this respect it cannot avoid running counter to the interests of a Church that had kept its faithful adherents purposefully ignorant regarding the way the universe really functions for over sixteen hundred years. This is not to suggest that scientists cannot be religious – many are. The difference lies in the fact that scientists are expected to keep their own religious beliefs away from empirical evidence.

Many of the Freemasons who founded the Royal Society in the seventeenth century and the French Academy of Sciences a few years later showed a strong religious conviction. To them the deity lay at the center of everything. One of the greatest scientists of all, Sir Isaac Newton (1642–1727), who is often referred to as the Father of Science, is typical of the men of his age. Newton is estimated to have written three or four times as many words trying to work out the dimensions of King Solomon's Temple than he ever did on scientific treaties. Yet this same man risked his own reputation and his very life in order to rid England of the Catholic King James II. Despite this, Newton was not a follower of the Protestant faith either. To Newton, and many of his peers, the deity lay at the very heart of all scientific endeavor. The unraveling of the mysteries of the universe did nothing to diminish the mystical presence that underpinned everything.

What Newton and men like him were not prepared to stand for was any earthly agency telling them what they should or should not believe. The legacy of the Cistercians and the Templars, which were both offshoots of the peculiar religious and political heresies that developed in Northern France, was an opening up of the world. International trade had given Western Europe access to new cultures. Many of these, like Islam, were more tolerant of scientific endeavor. The intended destruction of the Templars after 1307 could not put the genie back in the bottle. The inevitable result of post-Templar trade and exchange was the Renaissance, which in turn led to a rational examination of the world. Chief among those championing scientific investigation, universal investigation, and equality of opportunity were the Freemasons – the same men who formed the Royal Society and the French Academy of Science.

Since the Church could do nothing for the moment about Britain, it would try to strengthen its control over those States that were still Catholic. The stage was set for a bloody battle in which Freemasonry would lead the way.

CHAPTER TWELVE

THE SEEDS OF REVOLUTION

THE SEEDS OF REVOLUTION

Modern Freemasonry does its very best to keep a low profile within society. Its brothers are regularly reminded that their duty to the State in which they live and to their families must come before their commitment to the Craft. If by this behavior the leaders of Grand Lodge London, or those of any other Freemasonic body across the world, are trying to assure us that this has always been their position they are wasting their time. The truth is plain. Freemasonry led the way in taking the ideals of the Renaissance and the zeal of the Reformation and forging from these open rebellion and revolution. By so doing it could hardly fail to incur the further wrath of a Catholic Church that was already suspicious of its origins and intentions.

Nowhere was Freemasonry stronger in the eighteenth century than in the colonies of the British Empire in North America. First of all it has to be remembered that many of those who had traveled to America from Britain and the Continent in the early years of colonization had done so to escape tyranny in one form or another. Religious problems still beset a divided Europe, and Britain itself, from the sixteenth to the eighteenth century, see-sawed between Protestant and Catholic monarchs. Nobody with a belief that was in any way radical could feel safe in the Britain of the Tudors or the Stuarts and even those of very moderate beliefs were often persecuted.

Many traveled across the Atlantic. There, isolated from the home country by thousands of miles, a new series of social and political beliefs began to emerge. In the main these were fostered by the radicalism that was emerging within Britain itself, but which was often played out on an American stage. Most Americans probably breathed a sigh of relief when an end came to the religious uncertainty in the mother country and the Hanoverians came to the throne in 1714. If so, their enthusiasm was short lived because this dynasty itself began to make demands on the colonies that quickly became unacceptable.

It isn't so much the inevitability of the American Revolution that is fascinating. It was only ever going to be a matter of time before Americans would want to rule their own fortunes. Rather, it is the nature of the Revolution and the way it was fostered by a very specific type of Freemasonic belief that is of supreme interest. What is also significant is that a country that was a veritable hotbed of religious belief (after all, that is why so many people had come to America) quickly forged itself into a nation that absolutely refused to adhere to any apparent religious doctrine.

The build-up to the American War of Independence is well known. At the end of the wars against the French in Canada (Quebec had been taken in 1759), both Britain and the colonies were left in a fairly impoverished state. Wanting to recoup some of their investment the mother country began to impose ever more draconian taxes on the American colonies, which were met with ever strengthening resentment. The famous Boston Tea Party of 16 December 1773 is popularly cited as being the major flash-point for the American Revolution but, as in most significant historical events, things can rarely be put down to one specific event. The truth was that sparks were falling on the tinder of freedom in many places and the agency that seized the moment enthusiastically on both sides of the Atlantic was Freemasonry.

Nevertheless, the Boston Tea Party did come as a major irritant in worsening relations between America and Britain. Parliament had authorized the East India Tea Company to export half a million pounds of tea to the colonies. The usual taxes and duties imposed on tea by the British Government had been lifted in this case. The result would be that the tea could be sold within the American colonies at a price that would undercut even that of tea that had been smuggled ashore there. The British Government had committed a serious error of judgement. Their intention had been to try and salvage the ailing East India Tea Company but they had not realized, or did not care, that the strategy would seriously undermine the economy of the colonies.

On 16 December 1773, in Boston Harbor, three ships carrying cargoes of tea were attacked by colonists dressed as Mohawk Indians. As a result, 342 chests of tea were dumped into the harbor. It has been suggested that this was a deliberately provocative act and there is no doubt whatsoever that it was perpetrated by Freemasons. The raid on the ships had been arranged in a tavern called "The Green Dragon," a public house that had been purchased by St Andrews Lodge in 1764. St Andrews Lodge met there regularly, as did the Grand Lodge of Massachusetts. The "Mohawks" themselves remained anonymous – because to do anything else would probably have meant the gallows. There isn't any doubt, however, that the majority of them were Freemasons from St Andrews Lodge.

Freemasonry had come to America early and the first truly American Lodge was formed in Savannah, Georgia in 1734. As relations with the mother country gradually soured, so the Craft grew in importance and many new members were recruited in the years leading up to the American War of Independence. The first shots were fired in April 1775 and what turned out to be a bitter and acrimonious struggle dragged on officially until the signing of the Treaty of Versailles in 1783. One of the leading rebel generals was George Washington, who would go on to become the first President of the Unites States. He, like most of his contemporaries and many of his soldiers, was a brother Mason.

The actions of men like Washington had been spurred on by English radicals and specifically Thomas Paine. Paine was a son of Norfolk who, tiring of the low pay and hard working conditions in England, had shipped out to the colonies in 1774. There he showed his true political color and wrote *Common Sense*, the work that most inspired revolutionaries such as Paul Revere, John Adams, and George Washington. There is some ambiguity regarding Paine's Freemasonic credentials but if he wasn't a Freemason himself, he knew a great deal about the Craft. He wrote a long article entitled "The Origins of Freemasonry," which shows him coming down in favor both of its objectives and its secrecy.

During the War of Independence, American regiments and Lodges often went hand in hand. And when the war was over and a new nation was born, there was absolutely no doubt whatsoever, despite what is sometimes written to the contrary, that it was a nation based entirely on Freemasonic practice and principles. One of the major founding principles upon which the United States was to exist was that it should have no religious affiliation whatsoever. It was to be a secular State, though one heavily influenced by the peculiar religious beliefs of its leading founders. Evidence of this fact is to be found in the Bill of Rights and in many other places as the United States took its first tentative steps into independence.

The American Revolution was not an isolated event. Its origins lay back in the dawning of the Age of Enlightenment in the early eighteenth century. The names most associated with this departure in philosophy, science, and politics included many French thinkers. These included Descartes, Pascal, Bayle, Montesquieu, Voltaire, Diderot, and Rousseau. These people came from various regions of France but they all preached the new freedom that was eventually to spread across the world like a rash. And what do they hold in common? They were all either Freemasons or, in the case of the earlier examples, absolutely epitomized the Freemasonic ideal. Some commentators would suggest that this is not surprising, since Freemasonry was a "product" of the new enlightenment but it is equally possible that Freemasonry and its predecessors were "responsible" for that enlightenment.

The French Revolution would come a few years after the Americans freed themselves from British rule, but there was significant contact between revolutionaries in both countries. The same word was on the lips of both groups and the cry was Liberty!

Liberty is a Latin word and is derived from the Latin word for pouring, as, for example, wine. Modern etymologists suggest that this is because the feeling of liberty is akin to the sensation of being drunk but the truth of the situation is far stranger and more enlightening. Liberty is actually another name for the Goddess!

Deriving from early Roman times, Liberty, or more properly Libertas, was an important deity. Her origins probably lay in another goddess, this one part of the ancient Etruscan and Sabian pantheon. Her name was Feronia and she was the Goddess of the Dawn. Feronia in also a goddess of the earth and is directly associated with "Mania" another Etruscan earth goddess. According to some modern sources, Feronia and therefore Liberty can both be seen as merely alternative representations of Persephone, who in turn is synonymous with her mother Demeter and also the Egyptian Isis.

Both Liberty and Feronia were great friends to the poor and were especially associated with slaves who had gained their freedom. No wonder she became so popular in post-revolutionary America, where millions of the world's oppressed and impoverished came to find a democratic home. Liberty had many shrines and temples in ancient times, the first being dedicated in Rome as early as 300 BC.

Can it be a coincidence that Liberty was the watchword of both American and French revolutionaries in the eighteenth century and is also the name of a once revered goddess? Hardly, especially bearing in mind that in both America and France the revolutions were inspired and led by Masons. The proof lies in the many ways Liberty was displayed by the Freemasonic rulers of both countries, but especially the United States of America. The first definite appearance of Liberty as a goddess in America was thanks to Paul Revere, one of the organizers of the Boston Tea Party. He commissioned an obelisk dedicated to the Goddess Liberty at the time of the abolition of the Stamp Act in Boston in 1770. Revere was one of the Freemasons who met regularly at the Green Dragon in Boston.

Liberty, both as a concept and as a goddess, became so endemic to the new Unites States that she is to be seen everywhere. For example, she existed on many stamps, such as the intended five-dollar stamp shown below. Note the five-pointed stars at her brow. The importance of these will be explained in a later chapter.

In this representation Liberty wears the "cap of liberty" that has been associated with her since Roman times and which was the model for the caps worn by French revolutionaries.

Of course, the most famous representation of Liberty in the United States is so large that nobody could miss it, nor could they possibly doubt its Freemasonic origins. The Statue of Liberty towers to this day over Ellis Island in New York Harbor. It might surprise even some Americans to realize that this most famous symbol of American independence and of her once proud desire to encourage the world's struggling masses to immigrate to her shores is not American at all. The Statue of Liberty was a gift to the American people from their counterparts in France.

The Statue of Liberty was sculpted by Frederic Auguste Bartholdi, a prominent French sculptor and Freemason. The statue was originally designed for the opening of the Suez Canal, but it was decided that in order to celebrate the centenary of the American State, the giant figure should be constructed by public subscription in France and then shipped to the United States. The actual making of the statue was undertaken by Gustav Eiffel (1832–1923), another leading Freemason of his day and the man who would eventually create the Eiffel Tower.

Although built by French public subscription the statue was actually a gift from the Grand Orient Freemasons of France who represented the most ancient and elevated of French Masonic lodges.

If Freemasons today are somewhat reserved about their accomplishments, the same cannot be said to have been true of their nineteenth-century American counterparts. When the cornerstone for the plinth to support the statue was laid on 5 August 1884, the task was undertaken as a Freemasonic ritual, and conducted by Br. A Brodie, Grand Master of the New York Freemasons. Attending the ceremony were Masons from all around the world. The statue itself was shipped across from France and was dedicated on 28 October 1886 in another strongly Freemasonic ceremony.

How many people from all over the world regularly see photographs and drawings of this most remarkable modern marvel but never dream for a minute that the figure depicted has an ancestry that goes back for so many centuries. Nor do they realize that this is a structure dreamed up by, created by, and dedicated by Freemasons.

The statue of Liberty, one of the wonders of the New York skyline

Nor are Freemasonic Goddess-related activities in the United States restricted to edifices so large they cannot be ignored. There is evidence that an acknowledgement of the Goddess of the Craft was present at every step on the road to the creation of the Unites States of America.

The American declaration of independence was created and signed on 4 July 1776 but this document was nothing more than a statement of intent; an agreement between differing States that they would join together to fight against the perceived oppression of the British government. The United States did not become a republic until the signing of the American Constitution by 39 delegates from the various States that were to comprise the infant United States. The forging of the Constitution had been no simple matter. Delegates had gathered in Philadelphia from May 1787 and it took them until September to finally agree on the wording of the constitution. They gathered for the last time on 17 September, when all those present signed the finished document. Alerted by the planetary line-up at the time of the La Salette vision, I drew up an astrological chart for the day the American Constitution was signed. To my surprise I discovered that the sun, Mercury, and Venus had all been in the zodiac sign of Virgo on that most important day. Even more significantly, Venus was once again a morning star at that time. It stood 8° ahead of the sun. On the morning in question it would have stood blue-white and shining brightly in the growing light of the dawn. There was no moon in the sky at the time to obscure the glory of Venus. What is more, if the document was signed around the middle of the day, as seems to have been the case, the zodiac sign of Virgo was right overhead, in what is known as the mid-heaven position.

If all of this is not enough to convince skeptics that the day was specifically and deliberately chosen for this most important event, we should also bear in mind that this date, 17 September, has another very important significance. It is the day of the month on which the sacrifices were made at the Eleusinion in Athens, before those celebrating the Mysteries of Demeter set out for Eleusis. To clinch the situation it has to be remembered that a whole week was eventually set aside, though not until the twentieth century, to be called "Constitution Week." This covers the period from 17 September to 23 September, exactly the duration of the Eleusian Mysteries from the initial sacrifices until the completion of the Mystery itself.

Why should this be significant in terms of the American Constitution? It isn't difficult to see the connection. The Mysteries of Eleusis were all about a new birth and in a national sense that's exactly what the Constitution represented. It was a rebirth from the repression of colonial rule into the freedom of self-choice and independence. It was brought about by 39 men from the various States then in existence, but these were not just any individuals. By far the majority of them were either practicing Freemasons or would become Freemasons at a later date. It has been estimated that only five of the 39 delegates who signed the Constitution had no Freemasonic connection. We can be quite confident that there was nothing remotely arbitrary about the date chosen for the signing of the Constitution, and if readers are still not convinced, we might look at another very important "cornerstone" in American history – the Capitol building.

It can be argued that the Capitol building in Washington DC, is the most important building in the whole of the Unites States. While, for example, the White House offers a home and offices to the President of the USA, the President only governs by consent of the people and the place where those people make their decisions is in the Capitol. Similarly, buildings such as the Pentagon, also in Washington, also retain a symbolism and an importance of their own, but this too is subservient to the democratic will of the people, expressed by the House of Representatives and the Senate, which reside and make their decisions in the Capitol.

Recognized as being one of the finest examples of eighteenth-century classical architecture, in its finished form the Capitol owes much to ancient Greece and Rome. Of course, it only became possible to create a permanent home for the two houses of the American government once a site for the new capital city had been chosen. This took place around the year 1790, when the first President of the USA, George Washington, surveyed land on the border of Maryland and Virginia on the Potomac River in what is now known as the District of Columbia. This choice of location came as a result of bitter arguments between the Northern and Southern States as to where what was then known as the "Federal City" should be located. Was the final location chosen simply to appease the recalcitrant South, or is there more to it than that? It may be the most peculiar of coincidences but the fact that Washington DC straddles locations in both Maryland and Virginia could be deemed significant in itself, since the names of both States related directly to the hidden imperatives of Freemasonry, of which George Washington was a prominent brother. (Of course, the names of both these States already existed and had related specifically to British royalty – Queen Mary for Maryland, and Queen Elizabeth in the case of Virginia, but there may have been more to this in the minds of leading American Freemasons.)

The cornerstone of the Capitol was laid on 18 September 1793 in a ceremony that never pretended to be anything other than Masonic. A newspaper report at the time said:

> On Wednesday one of the grandest Masonic processions took place for the purpose of laying the cornerstone of the Capitol of the United States. About 10 o'clock, Lodge 9 of Maryland was visited by Lodge 22 of Virginia, with all their officers and Regalia. Directly afterwards appeared, on the Southern banks of the Grand River Potowmack, one of the finest companies of Volunteer Artillery that hath lately been seen, parading to receive the President of the United States, who shortly came in sight with his suite, to whom the Artillery paid their military honors. His Excellency and suite crossed the Potowmack, and was received in Maryland by the officers and brethren of No.22 Virginia, and No.9 Maryland, whom the President headed, and preceded by a band of music; the rear brought up by the Alexandria Volunteer Artillery, with grand solemnity of march, proceeded to the President's square, in the city of Washington, where they were met and saluted by No.14, of the city of Washington, in all their elegant badges and clothing.
>
> The procession then marched two abreast in the greatest solemn dignity, with music playing, drums beating, colors flying, and spectators rejoicing from the President's square to the Capitol in the city of Washington, where the Grand Marshal ordered a halt, and directed each file in the procession to incline two steps, one to the right, and one to the left, and face each other, which formed an hollow oblong square, through which the Grand Sword Bearer led the van, followed by the Grand Master P. T. on the left, the President of the United States in the center, and the Worshipful Master of No.22 Virginia on the right; all the other orders that composed the procession advanced in the reverse of their order of march from the President's square to the south-east corner of the Capitol, and the artillery filed off to a destined ground to display their maneuvers and discharge their cannon; the President of the United States, the Grand Master P. T ., and Worshipful Master of No.22 taking their stand to the east of a huge stone, and all the craft forming a circle westward. The cornerstone of the Capitol of the United States was then laid with appropriate Masonic Ceremonies.
>
> At frequent intervals volleys were discharged by the artillery. The ceremony ended in prayer. Masonic chaunting honors, and a fifteenth volley from the artillery.

A contemporary painting of President George Washington laying the cornerstone of the Capitol Building, Washington DC, 18 September 1793. Note President Washington's Freemasonic apron and that worn by the gentleman to the left of the picture.

Once again it seemed worthwhile taking a closer look at the date of this ceremony. Immediately we can see that the ceremony had been planned for 18 September, which was historically the date on which aspirants attending the Mystery ceremonies in Eleusis had undertaken the walk from Athens to Eleusis. As a result, we once again find the sun and Mercury to have been occupying the zodiac sign of Virgo on the appointed day. Venus was also a significant morning star at this time, rising a full 170 minutes before the sun.

(It is worth mentioning that Venus does not always appear as a morning star. Because Venus has an orbit inside that of the earth, when seen from our own planet, Venus periodically crosses the face of the sun. As a result Venus sometimes rises before the sun and at other times becomes an evening star, setting after the sun. In the case of all the examples I have quoted Venus was always a morning star and in Masonic terms this seems to have been an important factor.)

Why was Venus as a morning star so important to Freemasons generally and specifically to those who founded the United States of America? There are a host of possible answers. In ancient mythology, particularly that of the people of the Near and Middle East, Venus as a morning star represented one of the most important of their deities. To the Sumerians, from what is today Iraq, she was Inanna. Inanna had to journey to the underworld, where she was naked and without any form of defense. Later cultures called her Ishtar who, like Inanna, undertook a long and dangerous journey to the underworld. The purpose of her quest was to find and rescue her lover. There are strong parallels between both these stories and the Greek tale of Demeter entering Hades to rescue her daughter Persephone. There are also parallels with Demeter's resurrection of Dionysus. All are related to the earth's fertility cycles – the annual story of the death and rebirth of nature. At Eleusis, every aspirant symbolically took the journey to Hades and emerged, reborn, into his or her new life.

What can be in no doubt is that Freemasons as recently as the nineteenth century were arranging ceremonials that were to take place at astronomically significant times. They particularly favored the month of September, at which time the planet Venus occupied the zodiac sign of Virgo, the Virgin, and times when Venus was rising as a morning star ahead of the sun. This was true in the case of the signing of the United States Constitution and the laying of the cornerstone of the Capitol in Washington. The self same astronomical patterns had been present in 1846, when the Virgin Mary supposedly appeared to those two young shepherds in La Salette, France.

CHAPTER THIRTEEN

THE HIDDEN IMPERATIVE

THE HIDDEN IMPERATIVE

Because the United States now seems so wedded to Christianity, and is a hotbed of evangelical zeal, we might be forgiven for believing that it came out of the melting pot of revolution as a fully-fledged Christian country. Nothing could be further from the truth.

Any confusion regarding the motto "In God We Trust," which is now universally associated with the United States, can soon be dispelled. The original motto chosen by the first free Americans was "From Many, One." Only with the American Civil War did the new motto start to appear on coinage and eventually bank notes. This did not happen until 1864. The United States may not, at its inception, have been a "Godless" State, but it was one that clearly wanted to keep the deity at arm's length.

One of the first exponents of Independence and a man we have already looked at briefly was Thomas Paine. He is often referred to as the "Father of the American Revolution." This radical thinker and pamphleteer came to America from England in 1774. He rapidly threw himself into the colonists' cause. He was a man of firm conviction and, though he wasn't without personal religious belief, he made his feelings regarding Christianity well known. In his book *Common Sense* he said:

> As to religion, I hold it to be the indispensable duty of government to protect all conscientious protesters thereof, and I know of no other business government has to do therewith.

He also wrote in *The Age of Reason*:

> Whenever we read the obscene stories, the voluptuous debaucheries, the cruel and torturous executions, the unrelenting vindictiveness, with which more than half the Bible is filled, it would be more consistent that we called it the word of a demon, than the word of God. It is a history of wickedness, that has served to corrupt and brutalize mankind.

In the same work we find:

> I do not believe in the creed professed by the Jewish church, by the Roman church, by the Greek church, by the Turkish church, by the Protestant church, nor by any church that I know of... Each of those churches accuse the other of unbelief; and for my own part, I disbelieve them all.

Paine may not have been a Freemason, we simply don't know, but his views on the way a State should be run, freed from religious interference, played very much into the hands of the American Masons.

In 1789, George Washington, who was elected the first President of the United States in the same year, made his feelings on religion known in a letter to the United Baptist Churches of Virginia. He said:

> Every man ought to be protected in worshipping the Deity according to the dictates of his own conscience.

Benjamin Franklin, another founder of the United States, penned a letter to his friend, Richard Price. The letter was dated 1780 and said:

> When a Religion is good, I conceive it will support itself; and when it does not support itself, and God does not take care to support it so that its Professors are obliged to call for help of the Civil Power, it is a sign, I apprehend, of its being a bad one.

Both Washington and Franklin were committed Freemasons, as was James Madison, another leading revolutionary and a man who would become the fourth President of the United States, after having held high office from the start of the new nation. In his *work Memorial and Remonstrations Against Religious Assessments* in 1885 he had written:

> During almost fifteen centuries has the legal establishment of Christianity been on trial. What have been its fruits? More or less in all places, pride and indolence in the Clergy, ignorance and servility in the laity; in both, superstition, bigotry and persecution.

In the words of the First Amendment, taken from the Annals of Congress of June 1789, a document penned by Madison we find:

> The civil rights of none shall be abridged on account of religious belief or worship, nor shall any national religion be established, nor shall the full and equal rights of conscience be in any manner, or on any pretence, infringed.

Probably the man who had the most to say on this subject in a public sense was Thomas Jefferson, another leading revolutionary who became the third President of the United States. Jefferson may never have been a Freemason himself – again we simply don't know, but there is no doubt at all that he held a strong regard for the Craft, about which he spoke frequently. In a document from 1782 entitled *Notes on Virginia* he says:

> Is uniformity attainable? Millions of innocent men, women, and children, since the introduction of Christianity, have been burnt, tortured, fined, imprisoned; yet we have not advanced one inch towards uniformity. What has been the effect of coercion? To make one half the world fools and the other half hypocrites. To support roguery and error all over the earth.

There can be no doubt whatsoever that the United States, at its inception, was as radically opposed to interference in matters of State by the Church as would be the French after their own revolution. This is not at all the same thing as suggesting that the Founding Fathers were Godless atheists. Many of them were men of deeply held religious convictions, though there remains a sort of spiritual ambiguity among some of the most famous of them. Americans who are keen to show a direct connection between Freemasonry and devil worship find themselves in something of a difficult situation if they also wish to express their patriotism. People like George Washington, Benjamin Franklin, and Thomas Jefferson are heroes of American freedom. It was these men, together with their colleagues, who were mostly also Freemasons, and who set the seal on the foundation of the greatest State in the modern world. To suggest that they had diabolic tendencies is surely to sully the origin and good name of the United States?

The records of history clearly demonstrate that the revolutionaries of the United States and those of France were mutually supportive. However, in the case of France, the true causes of revolution lay in centuries of oppression on the part of the French crown, which was in close cahoots with the Catholic Church from at least the period of Charlemagne. When the time came, Freemasonic activity, open support from America, and the knowledge that the Americans had already gained themselves a republic led to a series of bloody events. These would eventually free France from both its monarchy and its dependence on the Church.

The possibility of revolution had existed in France for some time as the eighteenth century dragged on. The weak and not too bright King Louis XVI and his meddlesome, tactless queen, Marie Antoinette, inherited a seriously weakened economy when they came to the throne in 1774. Although the king struggled to find solutions, he could do nothing to silence the words of those intellectuals who were attacking the combination of Church and State. One particular man who by his writing is generally accepted as being an inspiration of the French Revolution was Voltaire (the pen name of Francois Marie Arouet).

Voltaire was a pamphleteer, an essayist, a playwright, and a philosopher. He was born in Paris in 1694 and soon after completing his education he was already in trouble with the authorities because of his radical beliefs. He was imprisoned in the Bastille for nearly a year and later had to flee France, living for three years in England. Although he came back to his home country in 1729, he found it impossible to live in Paris because of the criticism that attended him there. He wrote dozens of works on politics and social matters and later in life he became a great friend of Benjamin Franklin. Voltaire's views on religion were as complicated as those of Sir Isaac Newton, a man he greatly admired. Like Newton, Voltaire clearly believed in a higher power but he hated the stifling tendencies of orthodox religion. Voltaire was a Freemason, having been introduced to the Craft by Benjamin Franklin, but he was probably much more. As his death approached, Voltaire was certain that his outspoken attitudes regarding the Church would prevent him from being buried in consecrated ground. As it turned out this was not an issue. Within a few hours of his death in 1778 his body was removed from Paris and taken to, of all places, Champagne. There it was buried in the Abbey of Les Sellières, a Cistercian Monastery on the outskirts of Troyes!

This wasn't the end of the mystery. In 1791 the Revolutionary Government of France dug up Voltaire's body and laid it to rest with great ceremony in the Pantheon in Paris. In the middle of the nineteenth century the grave was opened, and the body had disappeared. It is also worth noting that the man often referred to as the "Father of the Revolution" spent much of his life living in Switzerland, the Templar State that had been founded during the fourteenth century. Where Voltaire rests now is anyone's guess – perhaps it is back in Champagne?

The Revolution was also much inspired by the writing of Jean-Jacques Rousseau, a radical freethinker and philosopher. Rousseau was another Freemason and had been born and raised in Switzerland! Like Voltaire, Rousseau maintained an unorthodox view of religion. He was opposed to what he saw as the tyranny of the Catholic Church and like the Revolutionaries in Paris called his personal deity "The Goddess of Reason."

The winter and spring of 1788 to 1789 brought crop failures and resultant shortages of grain for bread. Order began to break down, especially in Paris and this led to popular revolt. The first major event in the French Revolution was the storming of the Bastille, a notorious prison in Paris. This took place on 14 July 1789 and was led by a mob that had stolen rifles and ammunition from a government building earlier in the day. There is a persistent rumor that many of those taking part in the storming of the Bastille had been brought to Paris for this specific purpose and that they actually came from the South of France. An influential group of mostly intellectuals and businessmen had formed an association some time before the Revolution. They had become known as the "Jacobins." Many of the Jacobins were also members of the Grand Orient Lodge of France and it is they, and especially one of their number, the Freemasonic Duke of Orleans, who are specifically blamed for bringing matters to a head. When it looked as though the country was going to fall apart, a Revolutionary Council was formed. On 4 August 1789 it announced:

> Men are born and remain free and equal in rights. Social distinctions may be based only on common utility.

It wasn't very far at all from the American Declaration of Independence:

> We hold these Truths to be self-evident, that all Men are created equal, that they are endowed by their Creator with certain unalienable Rights, that among these are Life, Liberty and the Pursuit of Happiness.

The king survived for a while under the Revolutionary Government but he was eventually arrested and executed in 1792. What took place at this time was a bloodbath and was rightfully christened "The Terror." Many thousands of people were publicly executed. Aristocrats in particular, but also Church leaders, either fled abroad or were brought to account and the country dissolved into a horror that would only halt with the arrival on the scene of Napoleon Bonaparte in 1795.

The revolution in France was markedly different from that in America. While there had been those in America who did not support the war against Britain, the revolutionaries there could at least look toward a tangible enemy – the British government. In France things were different and the country had descended into a complicated and protracted civil war. It has long been suggested that Masonic-inspired groups such as the Jacobins were primarily responsible for what took place and there can be little doubt that the French Grand Orient was glad to see the back of both the monarch and the Church. However, if Grand Orient did ferment the original uprising, it lived to regret the fact because French Freemasons were themselves eventually banned for some time by the Revolutionary Government.

In the years following the bloody revolution, France took an excursion into empire under Napoleon Bonaparte and several times reinstated the monarchy. Only in the nineteenth century did France finally settle on republicanism. Throughout the whole struggle one figure predominated. She was the "Goddess of Reason," a figure who is also known in France to this day as Marianne.

It was in November 1793 that Christianity was officially abandoned in France, in favor of the "Goddess of Reason." To strike the point home a beautiful young actress, Mlle Malliard, was brought to Notre Dame Cathedral in Paris on 10 December 1793. (Notre Dame means Our Lady.) There, dressed in the robes of the Goddess, she was seated on the High Altar, where she lit a candle that was said to represent the light of reason. Of course to many this was seen as being nothing more than a mockery and an insult to Christianity but there were those present who would have seen things very differently.

The Goddess of Reason is no more an invention of revolution than was the goddess Liberty in America. The Goddess of Reason is simply an alternative name given to Athena, one of the most powerful of the deities in the Greek Pantheon. Athena was the favorite daughter of Zeus, King of the Gods. She had a special relationship with humanity, to whom she had taught farming, and she was the embodiment of wisdom. Most telling of all, Athena was a Virgin Goddess and was most probably the Greek mainland counterpart of the Great Goddess who had been of supreme importance to the Minoans. The French chose Athena for all these reasons but may have fixed upon her specifically because she was the patron goddess of Athens, where democracy first appeared.

Although in the early days of the Revolution Liberty, portrayed as a woman, also had a place, it wasn't long before the new Goddess of France took on a name. Marianne was officially recognized as early as 1792 when it was decreed that:

> the state seal was to be changed and should henceforth bear the figure of France in the guise of a woman dressed after the fashion of Antiquity,

standing upright, her right hand holding a pikestaff surmounted by a Phrygian bonnet, or Liberty bonnet, and her left hand resting on a bundle of arms: at her feet, a tiller.

Marianne in her martial guise

In later depictions Marianne gained a throne and a lion and also held the French flag. At her feet could be seen the code of law and the Declaration of the Rights of Man and the Citizen.

The name Marianne is of course a combination of the two forenames Mary and Anne. Mary needs no introduction but Anne is the name that Christian legend gives to the Virgin Mary's own mother.

After 1871 the founders of the Third Republic wanted to recreate Marianne in a form that would not inspire further insurrection and revolution. As a result, her Phryigian bonnet was abandoned and she was more commonly shown wearing a crown of wheat. In this form she has returned totally to the form of Demeter, or her Latin counterpart Ceres.

Marianne wearing the crown of wheat

A bust or statue of Marianne is now to be found in virtually every town hall in France. Her form is now simpler but she remains dear to the heart of the French.

It seems self-evident that the same relentless forces from Champagne and Northern Burgundy that had inspired the formation of the Cistercians and the Knights Templar still existed and scored a significant success in the eighteenth century. Although France is now the most vehemently secular country in Europe, the "hidden" Goddess who had been hugely important all along is now depicted in all the places where the French Republic serves its people on a daily basis.

This state of affairs follows a consistent pattern. From the eleventh century on Catholicism was maneuvered into presenting ever more glorious representations of the Virgin Mary in all its churches. To those "in the know" the meaning of her presence in the churches and cathedrals was obvious. However, when the time came to destroy the power of the Catholic Church in France, it would have been unthinkable to lose the Goddess as well. As a result she was recreated and now takes on a form much more like the one that would have been immediately recognizable to her devotees across the whole of Europe in ancient times.

The presence of the Goddess in every town and city hall, at the center of the democratic legislature, is no accident. It is what her supporters fought for across centuries. Far from being a secular State, France has now combined State and religion much more effectively than was ever the case under the crown and the Catholic Church. It is true that, to many, Marianne is nothing more than a symbol of their hard-won freedom but to those who are party to the secret she is much more.

The Vatican reeled as France threw off her Catholic past and sought to embrace a future without a State religion. But Rome was not about to let go of France easily. Vatican rulers throughout the nineteenth and twentieth centuries were certainly not blind to what had happened and, though the Church had been seriously wounded by the French Revolution, it was far from finished.

CHAPTER FOURTEEN

THE ALTA VENDITA

The Alta Vendita

Catholic history relates that "The Permanent Instructions of the Alta Vendita" came into the hands of Pope Gregory XVI around 1860. Although the Pope claimed to know who at least some of the authors of this extraordinary document were, he refused to name them. This may have been because one or more of them were responsible for the Pope obtaining the document. As a result, it might have been detrimental to the wellbeing of these individuals if he had named them directly. Of course, skeptics might equally justifiably comment that by keeping quiet regarding the authorship of the Alta Vendita Gregory XVI was merely concealing the fact that the document was a fiction, created by the Church itself.

The Alta Vendita was the highest lodge of an organization known as the "Carbonari," a group that was at its most powerful in Italy and France. The Carbonari, which means "charcoal burners" was a Masonic-like institution that was at its height in the early decades of the nineteenth century, though it claimed to have an ancestry that went back much further. As surely as orthodox Freemasonry stuck to the language and paraphernalia of stonemasons, so the Carbonari relied on expressions and ceremonies associated with charcoal burning. The place where members got together was known as the "baracca," which literally means "hut," while the interior of the meeting place was referred to as the "Vendita," which can be translated as the place where the charcoal was sold.

The similarities between the Carbonari and Freemasonry ran deep, so much so that any Third Degree Freemason would be welcomed into the Carbonari as a "Master," without any preliminaries at all. However, the Carbonari was far more politically motivated than Freemasonry, or at least became so with the passing of time. Like Masons, those joining the Carbonari had to pass through three degrees, which could not be undertaken in less than six months, and they also swore to horrible oaths relating to the retribution that would fall upon them if they divulged any of the secrets of their fraternity.

Paradoxically, bearing in mind what was to follow, the Carbonari were more religiously motivated than Freemasons. They were at least nominal Catholics and revered a patron saint, St Theobald[1] – something that the fanatically

---

1 St Theobald was the son of Count Arnoul of Champagne and was born in about 1061.

non-denominational Masons would never allow. The fact that they supposedly belonged to the Church did nothing to endear them to the Vatican, which is probably not surprising when one bears in mind the political turmoil of which the Carbonari were a part. The Carbonari had initiation ceremonies that differed very little from those of the Craft. It is reported that to be raised to the rank of Master, a member of the Carbonari had to undergo a ritualized version of Jesus' resurrection. The Church described this as being deliberately blasphemous. This sounds suspiciously like the raising of the Master in the Masonic Third Degree.

It is widely accepted that the lodges of the Carbonari fermented unrest and revolt in Naples and the Vatican States, as well as in Spain and France. Their political motivation came straight out of the desire for liberty, equality, and fraternity that had spawned the French Revolution and which had also led to the struggle for independence of the fledgling American States. The Church detested revolutionaries of this sort, particularly ones who created problems right outside the doors of the Vatican itself. Nevertheless, despite the protestations of orthodox Catholicism it was undoubtedly the actions of organizations such as the Carbonari that ultimately led to the existence of Italy as we know it today.

It may be unfair of the Catholic Church to lump together an overtly political organization such as the Carbonari with Freemasonry, though in the minds of those ruling the Vatican in the nineteenth century there was essentially no difference. As early as August 1814, two cardinals, Consalvi and Pacca, issued an edict, with the permission of the Pope, that said all Catholics must not, under threat of the severest penalty, join either the Carbonari or the Freemasons.

For several decades the name Carbonari became synonymous in Europe with armed insurrection and revolutionary ideals and it proved to be very popular in some circles far from Italy. The English poets Byron and Shelley both fought for and supported the Carbonari in their Italian struggles. By 1841 the organization seems to have been a spent force but it continued to exist for some time in France as the "Charbonnerie démocratique" an organization that was less violent but which sought to obtain a new republican constitution for France. The period during which "The Permanent Instructions of the Alta Vendita" was written seems to have been some time between 1820 and 1846, the latter of which was also the year of the La Salette vision.

The Alta Vendita is not a long document and I itemize below the sections of it that are most relevant.

Our Ultimate End is that of Voltaire and of the French Revolution – the final destruction of Catholicism and even of the Christian idea …

The Pope, whoever he is, will never come to the secret societies; it is up to the secret societies to take the first step toward the Church, with the aim of conquering both of them.

The task that we are going to undertake is not the work of a day, or of a month, or of a year; it may last several years, perhaps a century; but in our ranks the soldier dies and the struggle goes on.

We do not intend to win the Popes to our cause, to make them neophytes of our principles, propagators of our ideas. That would be a ridiculous dream; and if events turn out in some way, if cardinals or prelates, for example, of their own free will or by surprise, should enter into a part of our secrets, this is not at all an incentive for desiring their elevation to the See of Peter. That elevation would ruin us. Ambition alone would have led them to apostasy, the requirements of power would force them to sacrifice us. What we must ask for, what we should look for and wait for, as the Jews wait for the Messiah, is a Pope according to our needs ...

With that we shall march more securely toward the assault on the Church than with the pamphlets of our brethren in France and even the gold of England. Do you want to know the reason for this? It is that with this, in order to shatter the high rock on which God has built His Church, we no longer need Hannibalian vinegar, or need gunpowder, or even need our arms. We have the little finger of the successor of Peter engaged in the ploy, and this little finger is as good, for this crusade, as all the Urban IIs and all the Saint Bernards in Christendom.

We have no doubt that we will arrive at this supreme end of our efforts. But when? But how? The unknown is not yet revealed. Nevertheless, as nothing should turn us aside from the plan drawn up, and on the contrary everything should tend to this, as if as early as tomorrow success were going to crown the work that is barely sketched, we wish, in this instruction, which will remain secret for the mere initiates, to give the officials in the charge of the supreme Vente some advice that they should instill in all the brethren, in the form of instruction or of a memorandum ...

Now then, to assure ourselves a Pope of the required dimensions, it is a question first of shaping him ... for this Pope, a generation worthy of the reign we are dreaming of. Leave old people and those of a mature age aside; go to the youth, and if it is possible, even to the children ... You will contrive for yourselves, at little cost, a reputation as good Catholics and pure patriots.

This reputation will put access to our doctrines into the midst of the young clergy, as well as deeply into the monasteries. In a few years, by the force of things, this young clergy will have overrun all the functions; they will form the sovereign's council, they will be called to choose a Pontiff who should reign. And this Pontiff, like most of his contemporaries, will be necessarily more or less imbued with the Italian and humanitarian principles that we are going to begin to put into circulation. It is a small grain of black mustard that we are entrusting to the ground; but the sunshine of justice will develop it up to the highest power, and you will see one day what a rich harvest this small seed will produce.

In the path that we are laying out for our brethren, there are found great obstacles to conquer, difficulties of more than one kind to master. They will triumph over them by experience and by clearsightedness; but the goal is so splendid that it is important to put all the sails to the wind in order to reach it. You want to revolutionize Italy, look for the Pope whose portrait we have just drawn. You wish to establish the reign of the chosen ones on the throne of the prostitute of Babylon, let the Clergy march under your standard, always believing that they are marching under the banner of the apostolic keys. You intend to make the last vestige of tyrants and the oppressors disappear; lay your snares like Simon Bar-Jona; lay them in the sacristies, the seminaries, and the monasteries rather than at the bottom of the sea: and if you do not hurry, we promise you a catch more miraculous than his. The fisher of fish became the fisher of men; you will bring friends around the apostolic Chair. You will have preached a revolution in tiara and in cope, marching with the cross and the banner, a revolution that will need to be only a little bit urged on to set fire to the four corners of the world.

When I first came upon this document a few years ago it seemed to me to encapsulate everything I had come to know about the major conspiracy that had been taking place in France and elsewhere for at least a thousand years. How well it typified the observable actions of those people who so long ago had taken a definite decision to eventually put an end to tyranny – in both its secular and religious forms. In fact there was nothing remotely new about the suggested strategy outlined in the Alta Vendita document.

I have demonstrated the careful steps taken by the rulers of Champagne and Burgundy, right back to the eleventh century – these included getting their own Pope elected and fermenting a Crusade. The creation of the Cistercians and the

Knights Templar was also part of this strategy, while at the same time powerful international markets were established in Champagne. On no occasion did this remarkable group of people directly confront those they saw as tyrants. To do so would have meant losing everything for which they were struggling, because the ruling powers were too strong and too well entrenched. It has to be remembered that the Essene, and other revolutionary agencies within Palestine, had directly confronted the Roman authorities when they instigated the Jewish uprising of AD 70. As a result they had lost their homeland and been virtually destroyed. The lesson had been learned. It was better by far to infiltrate, to nudge, to coax, and to play the waiting game, for many generations if necessary. The whole rotten edifice of feudalism and the corrupt Church that was part of it could be persuaded to come crashing down of its own accord – if only the right 'mustard seeds' were planted.

The strategy of infiltrating the Church at its lowest levels, and then waiting for its operatives to slowly rise up the tree of power was nothing new at the time it was suggested by the Alta Vendita. It has been a constant process. In terms of people such as St Bernard of Clairvaux and the Popes he helped to create, the desire was for genuine power, which could be used to subvert Church beliefs and actions from the inside. The conspirators were opportunists and there were also times during which a slightly different policy was adopted. On occasions they used their influence to encourage the very worst candidates possible to climb the steps of the papal throne. The actions of these Popes, such as Pope Leo X, would naturally disgust a populace that was slowly growing in intelligence and the presence of the "rotten Popes" would lead to pivotal events such as the Reformation.

The actions of Pope Gregory XVI with regard to the Alta Vendita show that there was an understanding of what was taking place within the Church. Catholicism would not give up its power easily and it was likely to be well aware that the methods of the Alta Vendita were nothing new. The Church was built upon many centuries of manipulation and power. When it lost a battle it retrenched, considered the situation, and decided on ever-new policies to defeat what it knew to be "the enemy within."

Nowhere is this more obvious than in the method the Church used to fight against a continued elevation of the Virgin Mary within the Church at a grassroots level. Left unchecked this would eventually have brought her to the position of equality with God and Jesus.

After the worst excesses of revolution had died down, the Vatican clung tenaciously to its foothold in France. The new State might be secular in nature but it didn't try to prevent its citizens from practicing their own chosen religions.

Especially in rural areas Catholicism remained one of the major influences in the lives of the populace throughout much of the nineteenth century. But at the same time the Vatican was having to fight against the Goddess of Reason, the deity that became known as Marianne – whose very name was a clear allusion to two of the Church's most important female figures. Across France and beyond the inevitable connection was being made and as a result the Virgin Mary was growing stronger and stronger within the faith of the ordinary people. Instead of being a blessing to the Church, Mary was becoming something of a liability. She had to be put in her rightful place.

The Church had always claimed that Mary was a human being – a very special one but a human being all the same. Yet at the same time she was the Mother of God and was now even proclaimed "the Bride of Christ." The more overtly paternalistic characters within the Faith, God and Jesus, were being sidelined. This wasn't made any easier by the fact that the revolution in France had brought the importance of women within society to the fore. They now had a bigger voice and it was them who most regularly attended Mass and who retained the greatest veneration for the Virgin Mary. In France Mary, as Marianne, had become the Goddess of State while as the Virgin, her position within Catholicism seemed ambiguous and open to interpretation.

The vision of La Salette probably proved to be the last nail in a coffin lid that had to be fastened down permanently The Virgin of La Salette had openly criticized the priesthood and the leaders of the Church. The very fact of the vision added fuel to the fire of Marionology and led to specific actions on the part of the Vatican.

The ultimate response of Rome to the La Sallete vision can be seen in yet another vision of the Virgin Mary that took place at Lourdes, France in the spring of 1858. The story goes that a poor and sickly young girl, Bernadette Soubirous, had gone to a river near to her home in order to collect firewood. Bernadette was separated from her companions and became aware of a loud noise, like the rushing of wind or a storm, coming from a nearby grotto that was known as Massabielle. Peering into the cave Bernadette saw the form of a beautiful lady, who moved to the mouth of the grotto and stood by the side of a rose bush. Recognizing something holy and special, Bernadette fell to her knees and spoke the rosary, with the beautiful lady reciting the Lord's Prayer and the Gloria. After the prayers were finished the apparition disappeared.

During a two-month period that followed this first appearance, Bernadette saw the apparition a further eighteen times. According to tradition she had no idea that she was encountering the Blessed Virgin Mary until her very last appearance, which took place on 25 March 1858. At this time the vision uttered the words "I am the Immaculate Conception."

Lourdes is now one of the most visited holy sites in the world. In particular the sick and troubled go there to take the water that flows from the grotto in which Mary appeared. It is not my intention to pour scorn on the fervent beliefs of any individual, but there are aspects of the Lourdes vision that deserve scrutiny.

It has to be remembered that not long after the Vision of La Salette, the Pope had come into possession of the "secret" vouchsafed by the Virgin to Melanie Calvet. Melanie insisted that the Virgin had told her that the contents of the secret could be published in 1858. Those in the Vatican knew what the secret was and were aware of the scorn it poured on priests and bishops of the Church. In the intervening period the authorities in Rome had been far from idle. Four years earlier, in 1854, an official papal Bull had been passed declaring Mary's position as "the Immaculate Conception" to be canon law.

What does "immaculate conception" mean, and why might it have a bearing on the La Salette Vision? The fact that Mary was an immaculate conception means that, in the eyes of the Church, she was conceived without "original sin." Catholicism teaches that we are all born with original sin, as a consequence of Adam's fall from grace in the Garden of Eden. Because he ate the fruit from the tree of knowledge he was cast out of the Garden and the stain of his sin passed to the souls of all those born after him.

Although there is absolutely nothing in the Scriptures pointing directly to Mary being purged of the original sin that the rest of us have to bear, her sinless state had been discussed for many centuries. As early as the seventh century monasteries in Palestine celebrated a "Feast of the Immaculate Conception." The same feast appeared in England, in Winchester, before the Norman Conquest (1066). It was at first abolished by the Normans, who thought it to be a peculiarly Anglo-Saxon celebration, but was reinstated by St Anselm, who became Abbot of Bury St Edmunds in 1121.

There followed a great debate across Europe regarding the Feast of the Immaculate Conception. Interestingly enough, St Bernard of Clairvaux, leading light of the Cistercian Order and the main mover in the formation of the Knights Templar, was much opposed to the festival. His objections seem to have been on points of "timing." Bernard observed that there was an issue regarding whether or not Mary was without sin from the time of the conception of Jesus or if, rather, the birth of Mary should be considered the time at which she adopted this special position among humanity. In truth St Bernard was probably playing for time, or trying to prevent the Feast from taking place at all. It is my firm belief that he had his own reasons for not wishing the Immaculate Conception to ever be made canon law.

Arguments for and against the Feast of the Immaculate Conception came and went in the following centuries. Doubtless those who wished to believe that Mary was indeed born without sin held this belief sincerely and we find a peculiar situation in which those who were most committed to Mary, as for example was the case with St Bernard of Clairvaux, were the very people who were against the public and absolute proclamation of her Immaculate Conception. The reason for their objection is easy to see.

If Mary were ever to be declared officially by Rome to be an Immaculate Conception, the very act would scotch once and for all any question of Mary being a part of the Godhead. The removal of sin from her soul immediately confirms her as being a "creation" of God and in no way his equal. This, I believe, is the real reason why St Bernard was so against the doctrine and the Feast.

Of the fact that the Vision of La Salette had shaken the rulers of the Vatican there is no doubt. We have seen how hard Rome and its agents fought against accepting the La Salette apparition until it was forced to do so, partly as a result of the findings of successive inquiries but also because of public opinion. Within a few short years of 1846 tens of thousands of pilgrims were coming annually to La Salette. To deny the reality of the vision in the face of its grassroots popularity would have been pointless. But hanging over the head of the Vatican like the sword of Damocles was the fateful day, in 1858, when the secret vouchsafed to Melanie Calvet would be made public.

The adoration of Mary within France and beyond gained ground rapidly after her supposed 1846 appearance. Something had to be done in order to gain control of the situation and the Church responded. It pre-empted the publication of Melanie's secret by taking full command of the Virgin Mary, whose position within the Church had remained somewhat ambiguous for centuries. In 1854, as is stated by the *Catholic Encyclopaedia*:

> In the Constitution Ineffabilis Deus of 8 December, 1854 Pius IX pronounced and defined that the Blessed Virgin Mary "in the first instance of her conception, by a singular privilege and grace granted by God, in view of the merits of Jesus Christ the Savior of the human race, was preserved exempt from all stain of original sin."

After nearly 2,000 years Mary's position within the established Church was now written in stone. She could not be "as one" with God, or even with Jesus, because she was a "creation" of God. There is very little doubt that the Church hoped by this means to scotch at least some of the Marianist feeling that was prevailing at the time, which in turn had been fuelled greatly by the happening at La Salette.

This alone was not enough to prevent La Salette from becoming ever more popular to pilgrims from all around the world. What was needed was a bigger and better appearance of Mary that would marginalize La Salette and which would confirm, from Mary's own lips, that the latest dogma of the Church was accurate. This is precisely what the apparitions at Lourdes achieved.

I cannot comment on the apparitions from the point of view of Bernadette Soubirous. What she did or did not see in the grotto remains a mystery, since nobody but her saw any of the visitations of Mary. However, there are significant differences between the vision at La Salette and those that took place later at Lourdes. In the case of La Salette there were two witnesses, whose stories were identical. Neither of the witnesses faltered under cross-examination and both attested to the truth of what they had seen to their dying days. In addition, there was only one appearance of the Virgin Mary at La Salette – in other words no agency from the Church or elsewhere had any chance to influence what was taking place while it was happening.

This was certainly not the case at Lourdes. The first vision had taken place on 11 February 1858, but Bernadette saw the Virgin many times after that. Disbelieving her story, as had been the case at La Salette, the authorities, both Church and secular, had subjected the young woman to the same sort of interrogation that had been the lot of Melanie and Maximin. Some time before the last appearance of the Virgin, on 25 March, Bernadette had been taken to task by the priest of Lourdes, Dean Payramale, who had apparently told Bernadette that she must demand the name of the apparition and ask it to perform a miracle, such as making the rose bush at the entrance of the grotto bloom.

Obligingly, on 25 March, Bernadette went again to the grotto, where the Virgin appeared as before. Bernadette asked her politely, "Would you kindly tell me who you are?" After the question was repeated Bernadette got her answer as the vision said, "I am the Immaculate Conception, I want a chapel here."

Devotees claim that these words by the apparition prove conclusively that the vision of Lourdes must have been genuine. They observe that a poor, illiterate, and uneducated girl such as Bernadette could not have heard of the Immaculate Conception. This suggestion must surely be erroneous. The Immaculate

Conception had been made canon law four years earlier. Although Bernadette was poor, there is nothing to suggest that she had been brought up in a Godless family. In any case, such a long period of time elapsed between the first vision and the last that she was interviewed and questioned many times. She may well have been introduced to the term "Immaculate Conception" as it applied to the Virgin Mary during this period.

Whatever the truth of the situation, both Bernadette and the vision of Lourdes suited the Church wonderfully. Instead of spending the remainder of her life causing trouble for the Church, as Melanie Calvet was still doing, Bernadette, a naturally shy and retiring young woman, decided to become a nun. Her notoriety did nothing to prevent her from being harshly treated by the Mother Superior of her order, who believed that she might become vain and consider herself in some way special. Poor Bernadette, who was never strong, submitted humbly to any task that was given to her and remained totally obedient to her calling. She died on 16 April 1878, wracked in pain, her natural frailty having finally caught up with her. She was buried in the grounds of the convent for some years until, in 1908, her body was exhumed by the commission set up to inquire into her life. The body was found to be in remarkable condition and was eventually transferred to a glass reliquary within the convent chapel. Bernadette was pronounced a saint of the Catholic Church in 1933, her path to sainthood being a remarkable fifty years or so.

Bernadette Soubirous was everything that the irascible and moody Melanie Calvet or the restless and mercurial Maximin Giraud was not. Her meekness and submission after the events at Lourdes show how easy it would have been during the period of the visions for her to be influenced into "hearing" pronouncements from the Virgin of which the Church could wholeheartedly approve. At Lourdes, Mary had confirmed her position by declaring herself to be the Immaculate Conception, leaving those loyal to the Church, yet convinced of the divinity of the Virgin, with nowhere to go.

I looked at the Lourdes apparitions in the same way as I had done with the La Salette happening, drawing up astrological charts for all the days on which the Virgin Mary is said to have appeared. There is nothing remarkable about any of these charts. At the time, Venus was an evening star, in stark contrast to both La Salette and the pivotal moments in the history of the Unites States, such as the signing of the Constitution and the laying of the cornerstone of the Capitol. What is more, no planets were in the zodiac sign of Virgo during this period. This simple test may not contribute anything when it comes to forming a judgement of the veracity of the Lourdes apparitions but it indicates that the same eye for astronomical detail was certainly not present – either on the part of those deliberately creating a hoax or as a result of supernatural intervention.

But even Lourdes and its popularity, which soon eclipsed that of La Salette, was not enough for the Vatican. There was one further step it could take to ensure that Mary kept her place, though this did not happen until the twentieth century. The final piece of dogma that would fetter Mary to a corporeal body, created by God, was her Assumption into heaven.

There was a tradition in the Christian Church, dating back to at least the fifth century, that the Virgin Mary had not died and been buried in the normal way but that, because of her very special nature, her body was taken up, in its physical state, into heaven. A Feast of the Assumption of the Blessed Virgin Mary had been celebrated in Palestine even before the fifth century. There are, in fact, two versions of where the Assumption took place. Some legends say it happened in Jerusalem, while others point to Ephesus.

Local traditions and celebrations of the Assumption continued in various parts of the Christian world without any real interference from Rome until as recently as 1950, when Pope Pius XII declared infallibly that the Assumption of the Blessed Virgin Mary was a dogma of the Catholic faith.

Following on from this, the controversial Second Vatican Council of 1962 proved itself no less controversial by undoing part of the good work that the dogmas of the Immaculate Conception and that of Mary's Assumption had done. Although it still proclaimed the Immaculate Conception and the Assumption, its actual wording was:

> The Immaculate Virgin, preserved free from all stain of original sin, was taken up body and soul into heavenly glory, when her earthly life was over, and exalted by the Lord as Queen over all things.

So in the eyes of the Catholic Church Mary remains Queen of Heaven, but it appears that notions regarding her possible divinity are still being quashed by the Church, despite a tremendous groundswell of Marianism that perpetuates to the present time. There are still very active groups within the Catholic Church that constantly lobby for Mary to receive the badge of deity. Meanwhile, the reverence shown for her across the Catholic world has not diminished at all. Despite the Bulls passed by the Vatican Mary's actual position, in the hearts of her millions of followers if not in canon law, remains as ambiguous as it has always been.

Chapter Fifteen

The Pentacle – Darkness or Light

THE PENTACLE – DARKNESS OR LIGHT

In the world today there are an estimated five million Freemasons. This represents only a tiny proportion of Roman Catholics, who number over one billion. What is more, Catholic leaders are as vehement in their condemnation of Freemasonry today as they have ever been. Throughout most of the pontificate of Pope John Paul II, a German by the name of Cardinal Ratzinger was head of the Inquisition, that same institution that once tortured and burned anyone who was opposed to Catholic doctrine. In fact many believe that for much of John Paul II's time as Pope, Ratzinger was the real power behind the throne. Certainly it was his job to root out wrong practice and false doctrine within the Church. During his time as head of the Inquisition he never made any bones about his personal hatred for Freemasonry, or what Freemasonic membership meant to Catholics. As long ago as 1983 he declared publicly that:

> The faithful who enroll in Masonic associations are in a state of grave sin and may not receive Holy Communion ... Consequently, neither the excommunication nor the other penalties envisaged have been abrogated. (Cardinal Ratzinger, Sacred Congregation for the Doctrine of the Faith, 26 November 1983)

In April 2005, after the death of Pope John Paul II, Cardinal Joseph Ratzinger was elevated to the papacy as Pope Benedict XVI. As a result, Catholics who also wish to be Freemasons are clearly in for a hard time.

The Catholic Church is not alone in condemning Freemasonry. In particular, many evangelical Christian sects are opposed to its very existence. A cursory glance at the Internet will serve to satisfy interested parties that the Craft is probably under greater attack from Christians than has ever been the case. In response, most Freemasons keep silent, though there are quite a few Masonic websites that openly fight back, especially those originating in America.

The reasons the Catholic Church officially declares Freemasonry to be incompatible with its own teachings are many and varied. Briefly, the Church suggests that the secret nature of Freemasonry, together with its oaths, signs, and symbols all run contrary to Vatican teaching. Masons are accused of perverting those who are already Catholic by convincing them to take oaths and to make promises that they do not fully understand. It is further suggested that the secret nature of Freemasonry encourages those who are part of it to also associate themselves with other secret societies that are much more dangerous.

The Catholic Church also worries about what it calls the "unsectarian" nature of the Craft, which, it goes on to suggest, is actually "unchristian." It maintains that at the very least Freemasonry leads to "religious indifferentism" and brings a contempt for authority (presumably its own) that cannot be tolerated.

Cutting through the rhetoric, there isn't much doubt that the Catholic Church Fathers still hold Freemasonry in utter contempt and it is their firm belief that one of the goals of Freemasonry is to destroy the Catholic Church utterly. In the 1960s and 1970s there did seem to be some ambiguity regarding Freemasonic membership for Catholics. However, the remarks of Pope Benedict XVI, while still Cardinal Ratzinger, do not leave Catholic Freemasons much hope of an immediate reconciliation between the Lodges and the Vatican.

Meanwhile, a broad section of evangelicals accuse Freemasonry of every sort of crime imaginable. The worst of these is the assertion that Freemasonry amounts to Satanism. They suggest that Freemasons, knowingly or not, perform rites that are demonic in nature. Many of these assertions are specifically tied to some of the symbols that are prominent in the Craft. In particular, reference is made time and again to the Pentagram or Pentacle.

The terms "pentagram" and "pentacle" are interchangeable. Both refer to a five-pointed star of the sort shown below.

This symbol is so old it is impossible to know just how far back in time it actually extends. A pentacle similar to this is carved into a truly ancient standing stone on Ilkley Moore, Yorkshire, England. If it dates back to the quarrying and lifting of the stone the carving could have been put there five thousand years ago.

Of particular interest with regard to the pentacle in a modern sense is that it has attracted an association with witchcraft and, in particula, Satanism. It should be understood, however, that this is a very modern connection and owes nothing at all to the pentacle as it has appeared throughout history. Until the last century or so the pentacle was definitely not a symbol of evil. In the witch trials of the seventeenth and eighteenth centuries in both England and America the pentacle is never mentioned once and indeed it has, in its time, been as important to Christianity as it has to many of the world's many religions.

The first written evidence for the pentacle dates back to the time of the Sumerians, around 3000 BC. To the Sumerians the pentacle was associated with astronomy and with the Goddess Innana. Each of its points was delegated to a particular planet. These were Mercury, Mars, Jupiter, and Saturn, with the topmost point being reserved for Venus, the planet that was already referred to by the Sumerians as "Queen of Heaven." There could be a very good reason for this state of affairs and we will look at this more closely presently.

To the ancient Egyptians the pentacle had a specific meaning. When placed within a circle it represented the "duat" or afterlife. It was also representative of the "womb" of the earth, from which everyday life and the afterlife originated.

The Ancient Greeks, who were fascinated by all things mathematical, made little distinction between the world of the practical and that of the supernatural. The ancient Greek mystic and mathematician, Pythagoras saw in the pentacle a symbol for completeness and perfection. As a result the Pythagoras Mystery School referred to the pentacle as "Hugieia," which literally meant "health." Hugieia or Hygieia was also the name of a Greek goddess.

Hiding within the pentacle is a mathematical reality known as the "Golden Mean," something that would become especially important in medieval times. The Golden Mean is a mathematical proportion that tends to appear all over the natural world. It is a ratio of 1.618034, which is also known as Phi. It can be seen in situations as diverse as the growth ratio of a nautilus shell and the expansion of spiral galaxies far from earth. It also figures prominently in the proportions of the human body.

The Greeks knew about the Golden Mean and used it in the design of their temples and other buildings. They were aware that within the construct of the perfect pentacle the Golden Mean expressed itself time and again, as in the example below. The line from A to B is Phi of the line A to C, in other words it is 1.618034 times as long. Of course this relationship is repeated many times across the face of the pentacle.

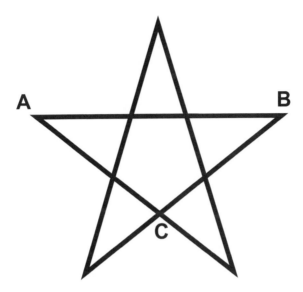

It was this observation that eventually led to the realization about Phi and the human body and is expressed well in the pentagram image of Heinrich Cornelius Agrippa. This became a specific fascination of the Renaissance world and was of particular interest to Leonard da Vinci.

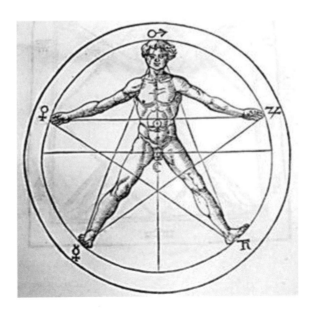

A follower and friend of Pythagoras, Pherecydes of Syros (circa sixth century BC) wrote a detailed work about the pentacle, which was entitled *Pentemychos*. This title refers to the five chambers or triangles contained within the figure. The Greeks had the strange idea that the pentemychos were also the chambers where the first precosmic beings had to be placed so that order could be created for the cosmos to take shape. They believed that the pentemychos lay within Tartaros, the great void that existed before anything else. It is a complex idea but the Pythagoreans seem to have believed that Tartaros continued to exist even after creation. Although everyone and everything was created from Tartaros and therefore the pentacle, in reality the pentacle was not apparent but at the "core" of all creation. The gateway between the world of the living and that of Tartaros was called "Krater." Krater is also a constellation of stars associated with the zodiac sign of Virgo and was seen in mythology as the "vagina" of Virgo – the gateway between life and death.

There is also a deliberate pun here because "Core" was one of the names of a Greek goddess who was synonymous with Persephone and also Demeter, both of whom had an association with the underworld and therefore Tartaros. One of the fruits that has always been considered sacred to the Goddess is the apple, and for a very important reason. If one cuts through the equator of an apple, or through its "core," the pattern of the pentacle will be seen within. This was a sound metaphor used by the Greeks to explain the relationship of the pentacle to the material and spiritual world.

The five-pointed star to be found within an apple

The pentacle was also significant to the Jews, and most certainly to their pre-Jewish ancestors. It denoted kingship but also had mystical overtones. In particular it was related to stories about King Solomon. The pentacle appeared on the "seal" of the City of Jerusalem in antiquity (even though Solomon's seal is now often shown with six points and not five).

To the ancient ancestors of the British and French, who were known as the Celts, and probably even to their predecessors, the pentacle represented the underground womb, from which all life emerged and to almost all civilizations the pentacle was used as a lucky charm.

The pentacle has very "human" proportions, which make it memorable. For example, its five angles have often been equated with the five fingers of the human hand. Alchemically they were associated with the four elements, fire, earth, air, and water, together with spirit. Early Christians referred to the pentacle as representing the five wounds of Christ, while the Jews used it to remember the five books of the Pentateuch.

Gypsies specifically refer to the pentacle as being representative of the Virgin and, like the Ancient Greeks, they demonstrate this by cutting an apple in half. To them, "Kore" is both the center of the apple and the name of the Virgin herself.

In Roman times the pentacle was the specific figure used by those involved in the building trade, which perhaps partly explains the importance it was to gain in Freemasonry. But it may have had an association with "Mithras," the deity at the center of a popular Roman religion mentioned earlier. Many Roman coins struck in the period immediately prior to Constantine's supposed conversion to Christianity carried the pentacle.

Throughout history the pentacle remained both mystical and a figure of great reverence, but despite what is generally known and accepted about the five-pointed star, there are other associations that have remained generally hidden and unknown to observers as a whole. I demonstrated some of these in *The Goddess, the Grail and the Lodge*.[1] Since time out of mind the flower that has been most commonly associated with the Goddess, and therefore ultimately with the Virgin Mary, is the common dog rose. This, I believe, was the case for several reasons. The dog rose is quite unusual in one respect. It can, like any other flower, be fertilized by passing insects, but if this does not take place, the dog rose is capable of fertilizing itself. In other words it personifies "virgin birth."

---

1 Alan Butler, The Goddess, the Grail and the Lodge, O Books, London, 2004.

It is my profound belief that this fact, together with the shape of the dog rose, also led to a connection between the dog rose and the pentacle, as show below.

I believe the connection between the rose and the pentacle exists because of the pentacle's direct association with the planet Venus and its movement through the heavens. There is a close mathematical connection between the orbital period of the earth and Venus. As seen from the earth the ratio is 5:8. The orbital period of the earth around the sun is 365.25 days, whereas the period of Venus, as viewed from the earth, is 583.9 days. Actually the orbital period of Venus is, in reality, 224.7 days but the fact that the earth is also orbiting the sun gives us a distorted perception of the true movements of Venus.

Eight periods of 365.25 days (earth) = 2,933 days
Five periods of 583.9 days (Venus) = 2,919 days

The two figures are within 14 days of each other, so the match is not absolute, but it is close enough to have attracted the attention of ancient astronomers.

If we look at things the other way round, using the true period of Venus we find the following:

Five periods of 365.25 days (earth) = 1826.25 days
Eight periods of 224.7 days (Venus) = 1797.6 days.

The relationships in this case is correct to within 29 days in five earth years.

In each case the result comes close to the definition of Phi. The true definition of Phi is 1.618034:1. In the case of our first example if we divide 583.9 by 365.25 we get 1.59863:1. In the second example, 365.25 divided by 224.7 brings us to 1.6255:1. Both are reasonably close assessments of the Phi ratio.

The physical shape of the rose also gives a good indication of the movements of Venus across the zodiac, when seen from the earth during five returns of Venus to the sun.

(As seen from the earth Venus passes the sun to become an evening star, in other words it rises after the sun. After a specific period it begins to fall back toward the sun, crosses the sun and then becomes a morning star – it rises ahead of the sun. This cycle is repeated time and again, but by the end of the fifth cycle, Venus will once again stand in the same part of the heavens it occupied at the start of the five cycles. This is the point at which the 5:8 ratio becomes apparent.)

Thus the pentacle becomes very important in terms of the movements of Venus as seen from the earth because this is the shape it describes within the zodiac across an eight-year period.

(Ever since Sumerian times that band of the heavens through which the sun, moon and planets appear to travel as viewed from earth, which is called the Plane of the Ecliptic, has been split into twelve sections. There are groups of stars within these sections, which have attracted specific names. These are the signs of the zodiac.)

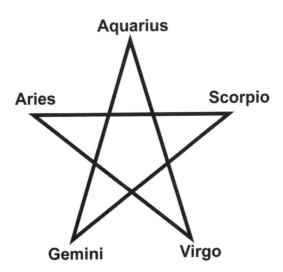

This figure represents a somewhat simplified version of the pentacle formed by the planet Venus as it crosses and re-crosses the surface of the sun, as seen from earth, during an eight-year period. In fact, the five Venus and eight earth cycle period is not exact, so the pentacle "slips" a little during each eight-year period, allowing the pentacle to move gradually around the zodiac.

This pentacle is never actually "seen." It can only be inferred and would have remained to ancient astronomers as one of the "mysteries" of the way Venus and the earth were tied together in a form of celestial harmony.

To Freemasons the five-pointed star or pentacle has always been of extreme significance. Its points are said to relate to the "five points of fellowship." Freemasons refer to the pentacle as the "blazing star." But within Freemasonry the pentacle is something of an enigma. It is never directly mentioned in Masonic practice and yet it appears time and again on Masonic regalia and as a decorative illustration. There is one exception to this state of affairs, because it was once common practice to use a lamp that shone a five-pointed star during the ritual of the third degree. It is mentioned in a letter from London in January 1815, which states:

> There is a small lamp used only in this Degree [3rd] whose light is seen from a Five pointed star.

Author Colin Dyer says, "The use of a small lamp in the form of a five-pointed star will be noted. It will also be remembered that this was one of the features deleted when the ritual came up for approval before Grand Lodge in June 1816."[2]

It would appear that the use of the blazing star during the third degree ritual ceased at a time when the pentacle was beginning to be the focus of less than favorable attention. By this period the pentacle was attracting overtones of the occult and Satanism.

There are many places from which Freemasonry may have drawn the pentacle. First of all it was of Pythagorean interest and it has often been suggested the Freemasonry attracted its fascination for geometry from Pythagorean and therefore generally Greek sources.

The five-pointed star was known as the "Seal of Solomon," even before the six-pointed variety had more commonly attracted this name. I have mentioned the fascination Masons have for Solomon and his works time and again.

The pentacle was also significant to the Knights Templar, who used the figure repeatedly, possibly partly because of its own association with Solomon. Since Freemasonry is generally accepted as drawing much from Templarism, the pentacle could have passed to the Craft from this direction.

---

2 Ars Quatuor Coronatorum, vol. lxxxix (1976), pp. 202-3.

It is also a fact that all members of old Masonic guilds had their own "masons' mark," something that distinguished their own work and set it apart from that of other stonemasons. This was necessary both for quality control and as a method of assessing the payment due to any mason. These marks can be seen all over castles and church buildings throughout Europe and beyond. The pentacle was a frequently used device with this regard.

A copy of a stonemasons mark in the shape of a pentacle from Rosslyn Chapel, Scotland

The pentacle also had a hidden use to masons, especially around the time of the Knights Templar and after, when the "Gothic" form of architecture based on the ogive was beginning to spread across Christendom.

There was one way a medieval architect/stonemason could produce a perfect ogive. This was by wrapping the figure around a pentacle, as shown below:

The implication is that the same Phi relationships inherent within the pentacle were passed directly to the arch, which itself became a Phi figure. Thus, although the pentacle has become a symbol of some embarrassment to Christianity in the last couple of centuries, its form, in theory at least, was responsible for the most magnificent buildings Christian masons ever created.

Despite the loss of the Third Degree Lamp, the pentacle retains its importance to Freemasonry even now, even if this is somewhat played down these days. Certainly in the eighteenth century there was no problem at all regarding its use. This is especially noticeable in the foundation of the United States, which as we have seen was a process undertaken almost entirely by those of a Freemasonic persuasion.

The greatest of the first Americans was undoubtedly George Washington, who was also of course a Mason. The five-pointed star formed a part of the heraldic crest of the ancient Washington family.

Like all Masons, during ceremonies Washington wore an apron. These are often made of sheepskin and in a ritual sense they take the place of the more robust leather aprons stonemasons would have worn for their work. In the case of Freemasonic aprons, these generally carry rich patterns of symbols related to the Craft. Below is a picture of a Masonic apron worn by George Washington. This one was made of white silk and had been presented to Washington in 1784. It carries a wealth of Masonic symbolism, among which, down toward the bottom right-hand side, can be seen the pentacle. The apron was given to George Washington by the Marquis de Lafayette, a Freemasonic French nobleman who fought for the Americans in their war of independence and who went on to make the original designs for the layout of Washington DC.

The pentacle lay at the very heart of the creation of the United States of America, which of course is not surprising when one bears in mind how many Freemasons held power at the time. As a five-pointed star it is to be seen on the American flag and it also figures prominently on the Great Seal of America and on United States currency and stamps. In at least one case the five-pointed stars are arranged as a diadem around the brows of Liberty herself.

Researchers argue that the situation goes much further than this. La Fayette, the man who laid out the street plan of Washington, almost certainly "hid" the pentacle within his designs. The pentacle in this case is of the "one point down" variety, with the lower point resting on the White House.

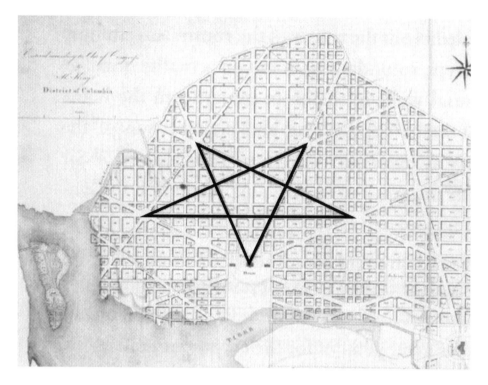

A copy of an old street map of Washington dc, with the pentacle superimposed upon it. The lower point of the pentacle marks the position of the White House.

When we bear in mind the hidden religious imperatives of Freemasonry that I have detailed time and again in this book, it is not remotely surprising that a country dedicated to the "Goddess of Liberty" was so keen to show its affiliation to a symbol that has always been within the province of Venus and the Goddess as a whole.

What is rather more surprising is that a geometric device such as the pentacle, that has such an ancient and illustrious past, should now be used as one of the sticks that critics use to beat the Craft. The critics seem to forget that the pentacle was, for a long time, also of singular importance to Christians. The accusations regarding the pentacle and its use as a "proof" that Freemasonry is essentially "Satanic" in nature can be seen in a wealth of books and all over the Internet. This state of affairs is all thanks to one man. His name was Eliphas Levi and he lived from 1810 until 1875.

Eliphas Levi, whose real name was Alphonse Louis Constant, was born in Paris, the son of a fairly poor family. He was a clever boy and eventually managed to gain admission to a seminary, with the intention of becoming a priest.

Constant soon became interested in the occult. He had radical left-wing views and maintained his own particular ideas about chastity, so that although he was eventually ordained as a priest, he was soon dismissed from his calling. In 1846, the same year as the La Salette vision, Constant met and married Neomie Cadot, who at the time was only 17 years of age. The marriage was not a success and was eventually annulled in 1865. Constant earned a good living in journalism but was growing ever more committed to his occult interests. It was around this time he changed his name to Eliphas Levi.

In 1861 Levi left journalism for the world of book writing. He created his first book, which was entitled *The Dogma and Ritual of High Magic*. This was quickly followed by *A History of Magic*, *Transcendental Magic*, and *The Key of Great Mysteries*. It was in these works that Constant introduced his audience to what he claimed was the true importance of the pentacle as it related to magic. When the pentacle was placed point down, he claimed it had a Satanic quality and was associated with the form of a goat, which most people these days equate with the devil. A picture of the goat and pentacle as it appeared on a Tarot card in a pack inspired by Constant is shown below.

Because "Wiccans," the name given to followers of witchcraft, gradually began to use the pentacle in their own religious practices, the pentacle began to lose its Christian and other connections and became associated in the public mind with something dark and sinister. All of this probably came about in the first place because of a simple misunderstanding associated with the figure known as "Lucifer."

The explanation for what Lucifer actually represents is to be found in *Funk & Wagnalls Encyclopedia*. It says:

LUCIFER or PHOSPHORUS (the Light Bearer) in classical mythology, the name for the planet Venus as the morning star; the planet was personified (by the Greeks) as a youth, the son of the dawn goddess Eos, and the brother of Vesper, or Hesparus, the evening star. A verse in Isaiah 14:12 alludes to the King of Babylon as "Lucifer, son of the morning"; in the belief that this verse contained a reference to the fall of Satan from Heaven, the fathers of the early Christian church attached the name Lucifer to Satan.[3]

This confusion led to the insertion of the name "Lucifer" in specific sections of the King James version of the Bible that elude to Satan. However, Lucifer, in another guise, appears as a Christian heroine. St Lucia, or Lucy, is a fairly obscure third-century saint from Sicily, who committed her virginity to God, but who was sold into marriage by her parents. She was eventually martyred and her relics were revered by the early Church. Devotion to St Lucy is especially strong in Sweden, where she seems to have become attached to an already existent pagan celebration. Even in her Christian guise her feast day was originally on the shortest day of the year in December, but the reformation of the calendar saw it eventually being celebrated on 13 December. To this day in villages and towns all over Sweden, in the very early hours of 13 December a young woman (a virgin) dressed in white, goes from farm to farm or house to house. She wears a crown composed of lingonberry twigs and burning candles and is called "the Lucy Bride." The Lucy Bride brings gifts of saffron cakes and coffee.

Nobody denies that St Lucy, at least in the way she is celebrated in Sweden, harks back to the old pre-Christian midwinter solstice celebrations. Venus appearing as a bright morning star would act as a herald to the first sun of the New Year and therefore would be a messenger of the end of winter. Despite this certain fact, nobody equates St Lucy with the devil.

Nevertheless, the writings of Eliphas Levi, together with the behavior of certain Freemason/Occultists, particularly in nineteenth-century France, has caused the pentacle to gain Satanic overtones that unjustly predominate in the public psyche.

---

3 Funk and Wagnalls, Funk and Wagnalls Enclyclopedia, Hammond and World Atlas Corp, Union, New Jersey 1984.

It has been suggested that the goat figure supposedly associated with the pentacle may well be the character referred to by the Knights Templar as "Baphomet." At the time of the Templar trials after 1307 one of the accusations brought against the Templars is that they worshiped a mysterious "bearded head" whom they called Baphomet. There is nothing in the accusations of the time to suggest that this head was a goat or even that it was Satanic in nature. Neither was there anything said during the trails of the Templars to associate Baphomet with the pentacle. In fact, Baphomet has now been shown to be a word written in a biblical cipher known as the Atbash Cipher. The bearded head and the word Baphomet are most likely not related because Baphomet actually means "Sophia," which is a feminine concept and most probably refers to the Templars reverence for the feminine in religion.

Despite being somewhat played down these days, the pentacle or blazing star remains central to Freemasonry all over the world. It is repeatedly and emphatically enshrined in the symbols of the first truly Masonic State ever to be created, which is of course the United States of America. Why? Because the pentacle is significant mathematically, culturally, and religiously. At the same time it is suitably ambiguous. To most Masons its five points merely represent the five points of fellowship, while to those who have studied the importance of geometry to the Craft it takes on a different and more practical meaning. Finally, to those Masons who "really" know, the pentacle is the enduring symbol of the Goddess, whose worship has been important to the inner sanctum of Freemasonry since its inception and long before to its founding institutions.

Chapter Sixteen

London and the Goddess of Britain

LONDON AND THE GODDESS OF BRITAIN

During the last few years I have spoken to groups of Freemasons all over Britain, as well as talking to them individually. During this time not one Freemason has ever openly admitted to me that he was aware of the deep elements of Goddess worship that lie at the heart of the Craft. Of course, parts of Freemasonic knowledge and ritual are, by their very nature, secret, which might preclude me, as a non-Mason, from being "put in the picture" and this is an impression that I definitely get from high-ranking Masons. At the same time I have been told by leading Scottish Freemasons that there are specific references to the Virgin Mary within the higher degrees of Scottish Rite Freemasonry, if one knows where to look for them.

It is just possible that the relationship between Freemasonry and Virgin or Goddess worship has now been totally forgotten by individual Masons, though this certainly was not the case as recently as the nineteenth century. Evidence of this comes from the pen of the British novelist Anthony Trollope. Trollope was born in 1815 in London, the son of a barrister who eventually fell on hard times. Young Anthony managed to flourish in the face of adversity and eventually secured a position in the British Post Office, ultimately climbing the ladder to a high-ranking post. Outside of his books Trollope is probably best remembered as being the inventor of the post box. But his first love was writing and he eventually penned 47 novels, some of which have become classics of English literature.

Anthony Trollope was a respected Freemason, having been raised to the Craft in 1841 in Banagher, Ireland. There are frequent allusions to Freemasonry in Trollope's books but none is more compelling than a description he gives of a character in his novel *Barchester Towers*, which was written in 1857. The text leads us to believe that this individual, Mr. Thorne, is himself a Freemason, but he is clearly much more. In one section Trollope says:

> He, however, and others around him, who still maintained the same staunch principles of protection – men like himself, who were too true to flinch at the cry of a mob – had their own way of consoling themselves. They were, and felt themselves to be, the only true depositories left of certain Eleusinian Mysteries, of certain deep and wondrous services of worship by which alone the gods could be rightly approached. To them and

them only was it now given to know these things, and to perpetuate them, if that might still be done, by the careful and secret education of their children.

We have read how private and peculiar forms of worship have been carried on from age to age in families, which to the outer world have apparently adhered to the services of some ordinary church. And so it was by degrees with Mr. Thorne. He learned at length to listen calmly while protection was talked of as a thing dead, although he knew within himself that it was still quick with a mystic life. Nor was he without a certain pleasure that such knowledge, though given to him, should be debarred from the multitude.[1]

Readers will recall the parallels I have drawn between Freemasonry and the ancient Mystery Rites celebrated at Eleusis in Greece. In this passage Trollope specifically mentions "Eleusinian Mysteries." He indicates that Mr. Thorne believes himself (and others) to be "the true depositories" of these Mysteries. Mr. Thorne is shown to be from a family that has, for generations, practiced "private and peculiar forms of worship" but that they have always apparently "adhered to the services of some ordinary church."

There could be no better description than this of someone who retains a view of Freemasonry that acknowledges its truly ancient origins, its secrecy, and its careful protection, generation to generation. Of course, Mr. Thorne is a fictional character, but he emanates from the pen of a known Freemason, Anthony Trollope. This whole passage about Mr. Thorne would be passed over by any average reader without a second thought, but when one is in possession of the facts, its implications are amazing.

Anthony Trollope was extremely successful and he rubbed shoulders with the literary intelligentsia of his day. He was well traveled and visited the United States, in 1861 and 1868, where he would undoubtedly have mixed with American Freemasons, though there were also strong American connections with his family that dated back to as early as 1830. There is no doubt in my mind that his description of Mr. Thorne indicates that Trollope knew very well of a surviving

---

1 Anthony Trollope, Barchester Towers, 1857, London, Chapter 22.

religious and political imperative that was extremely ancient, and that had its origins in the Mysteries of Demeter, which arose in Ancient Greece.

I carried out an in-depth appraisal of what is known of Anthony Trollope's own religious beliefs. He was from a family that supported the High Church of England, but in the end his own religious leanings are probably best summed up by Michael Mayne, who wrote a much later introduction to *Clergymen of the Church of England*, a book by Anthony Trollope that was first published in 1866.

Trollope was not a Catholic but a member of the High Church of England. Michael Mayne talks of Trollope as having "tolerance within a broad spectrum of belief and interpretation; a high regard for the individual conscience," which itself shows his Masonic leanings. It is known that Trollope had significant sympathy with a group known as the "Oxford Movement," a religious imperative within the Church of England that gained ground while Trollope was in his late teens and early twenties. The Oxford Movement sought to bring back much of what had been lost to Anglicanism when it divorced itself from Rome. However, the Oxford Movement itself was shot through with Freemasons, many of whom may have been trying to build bridges with Rome in order to alter Catholicism in the way the authors of the Alta Vendita sought to do.

The Britain of Trollope and his counterparts had fared much better than France in that it had managed to avoid the bloody revolution that burned across the streets of Paris and other French cities. The reasons for this are complex and certainly do not reflect any lack of revolutionary zeal within the British. There were political reformers and agitators aplenty – after all some of them, like Thomas Paine, were partly responsible for the American break with Britain and yet others took an active part in the French Revolution. But somehow, and against all the odds, successive governments in Britain managed to avoid the ultimate confrontations with the middle classes that lay at the heart of popular revolutions such as that experienced in France.

The English Civil War of the seventeenth century offered some solace to those who opposed the power of the monarchy, while the iron grip of Rome had been shaken off even earlier, during the Reformation of the sixteenth century. Once Catholicism allied to the State had been made impossible in Britain after the ousting of King James II, the sort of revolution that came to destroy the monarchy of France probably looked less and less likely. It is also true that the Anglican Church never had the same political clout or influence as did Rome Catholicism on the Continent. Nonconformists made up an increasingly large part of the population and Britain became a land of religious toleration. Also, in the words of Napoleon, Britain was a nation of shopkeepers. Although there was still abject poverty, people generally were getting a slightly bigger slice of the national cake and under these circumstances revolution may not have looked too attractive.

This did not mean that Freemasonic zeal was any less intense in Britain – it merely manifested itself in different ways. Those who had spawned Templarism and ultimately Freemasonry had their own particular religious beliefs, as is demonstrated by Anthony Trollope's Mr. Thorne. However, they also held to very particular ideals regarding personal freedom and democracy. By the seventeenth century the monarchs of Britain had been effectively stripped of any real power, while the various churches and chapels did little or nothing to control an increasingly democratic parliament.

The Goddess had been conspicuous by her absence in Britain during and immediately after the English Civil War (1642–1648). At this time High Anglicanism, which still showed a reverence for the Virgin Mary, was purged by a new Puritan zeal. Puritan churches were stark affairs, with no stained glass or iconography of any sort. It wasn't until the restoration of the monarchy and the arrival of King Charles II in 1660 that Freemasons with the same knowledge as Mr. Thorne could reinstate the Goddess. When they did so, they chose a model not dissimilar to that eventually used in France and one whose use tells its own fascinating tale.

Not long into the reign of Charles II, who was probably a Freemason himself, as had been his father and grandfather, the figure of Britannia was resurrected from Britain's ancient history. She became everything to the British that Marianne would be across the Channel.

Britannia was the name of a goddess who had been worshiped in Britain during the time the Romans were in the Islands. She had appeared on the coinage of the Emperor Antoninus Pius in the second century and the choice of a goddess associated with this emperor was no coincidence. Almost unique among Roman emperors of the time, Antoninus Pius was a man who could be deeply admired. He might, to the seventeenth-century British mind, have represented the ideal leader and someone who, knowingly or not, practiced Freemasonic ideals.

Antoninus Pius showed the greatest concern for his subjects across the empire. He had a kindly disposition, was well trained to the office of emperor, made sure he knew what was going on in all parts of his domains, and above all he was generous. Instead of raping the empire at times of financial austerity, he emptied his own coffers. Antoninus also overhauled the laws of the empire and did much to help both the poor and slaves, giving them rights that would have been unthinkable under any other emperor. Of Antoninus' own religious beliefs we know little, except that he lived an abstemious and simple life and that he had a great respect for philosophy. He may well have been involved in the cult of Mithras but there is no absolute proof of this. It is also a fact that Christians suffered less during his reign than they did before or after and that he showed great tolerance for the religious preferences of the many nations that fell under his control. It is no coincidence that the reign of Antoninus Pius (AD 138–161) was one of the most peaceful periods the Roman Empire ever experienced.

If Britannia was the counterpart of a Roman goddess, we cannot be certain which one she represented. It is far more likely that she owed her existence to a very important native British goddess, whose name was Brigantia. Brigantia's name means "High One" and she was in almost every sense a British counterpart of the Egyptian Isis or the Greek Demeter. She had a special affinity with flocks, cattle, water, healing, victory, birth, and death.

Both Brigantia and Britannia also owe something to an even older British goddess whose name was Brid. Brid was one of the great Mother goddesses of Ireland but was also revered in Wales and other parts of Britain. Brid was the goddess of fertility, fire, all feminine arts and crafts, and also the martial arts. She was also responsible for healing, agriculture, all learning, love, witchcraft, and knowledge of hidden things. When Christianity came to the British Isles Brid was too powerful to be instantly forgotten. Her memory was subsumed into the figure of the Virgin Mary but she also took her place in the host of saints as St Bridget.

Coin of Antoninus Pius (ad 136–161) showing Britannia

Britannia was forgotten for a long time, or at least her image has not come to light. She did turn up briefly as a personification of the English Queen Elizabeth I (1533–1603) and was often thought of as synonymous with the Virgin Queen.

Unfortunately we have no record as to whose actual idea it was to resurrect the form of Britannia during the reign of Charles II, but the king must have been close to the idea himself because one of his mistresses, Frances Stuart, became the model used on the first modern coin minted that carried Britannia's image. The most likely candidate is probably Sir Christopher Wren, not only a high-ranking Freemason but also a founder member of the Royal Society.

A farthing of 1672. The first coin in modern times to show Britannia.

Charles' Britannia coins were created by Philip Roettier, possibly aided by his brothers John and Joseph. All three had been employed at the London mint. Whoever created the design was certainly familiar with the coins of Antoninus because there are many similarities. However, there are also differences. On the Roetttier coin Britannia sits alongside a shield that carries the Union flag, and in her right hand she holds a sprig of foliage. This foliage looks uncannily like the acacia held in the hand of the "Beautiful Virgin of the Third Degree."

Britannia was immediately very popular. The Bank of England, which was created in 1694, chose her for its own image and she became inextricably linked with the rising success of Britain as a nation. Her form has appeared on and off on both banknotes and coins in Britain ever since.

In this medal Britannia looks much more like Demeter. She has lost her martial aspects and carries foliage and a horn of plenty.

A patriotic nineteenth-century statue of Britannia from Hull, England

Britannia is a common name for public houses in Britain

In the use of Britannia, as with the French Marianne and the American Liberty, we can detect the deliberate duplicity that attends goddess figures in many countries. To the vast majority of people these are nothing more than abstract, emotional images, depictions of the "Mother Country." All have been used in times of war to raise a sense of patriotism but they all carry the attributes of very ancient goddesses. It is my contention that their presence is in no way arbitrary and that they have all been created by the same group of religious heretics that was responsible for the Knights Templar and for Freemasonry. At the very least they serve a psychological need within humanity that is not addressed by the patriarchal nature of modern religions.

Nowhere is Britannia more important than at the heart of that most peculiar of institutions, the City of London, a place that would become more intimately associated with both Freemasonry and the building of the modern world than any other city on the globe.

The City of London is quite different from the area that is better understood as "Greater London." Occupying only about one square mile it forms what is certainly the most prosperous and influential area to be found anywhere in the world. The City of London has a resident population of about 7,000 people but its working population is closer to 300,000, the majority of whom arrive and leave on a daily basis. Over the years the City has acquired a unique political status and stands quite independent of the Government of Britain as a whole.

While all other areas of Britain are subject to a form of democracy that sees individuals voting for representatives who sit on town and city councils, the City is administered by a body known as the Corporation of London. The Corporation of London includes the Lord Mayor, who is elected annually, the Court of Aldermen, and the Court of Common Council. Aldermen govern a particular ward and are also elected, though in this case every six years.

The voting system in the City of London is quite different from that of anywhere else in Britain. Each body or organization within London, whether incorporated or unincorporated, has the right to supply voters. These may be British, from the European Union or the Commonwealth and either resident or appointed. It is not necessary to live in the City in order to have voting rights and this is where it differs significantly from the rest of Britain.

The "wards" or political divisions of the City are 25 in number. Each ward elects one alderman and a number of councilors, according to the size of the ward.

There are over 100 livery companies in London. The livery companies are an ancient institution and it is generally thought that their role is ceremonial but this is not the case. A group of senior liverymen form an organization known as Common Hall. It is from within Common Hall that the Lord Mayor and the Sheriffs are elected. In addition to Common Hall, there is also the Court of Common Council. Those who sit within Common Council are individuals who have been voted into their positions within the wards of the City. Although voters do not have to reside in the City, those who qualify for Common Council must hold a freehold or leasehold in the City, have resided there for at least a year, or be Freemen of the City.

The Lord Mayor and the Sheriffs who assist him are the most powerful figures in the City. They are voted into office each year. After the Mayor is elected in September he takes office in November, at which time the Lord Mayor's Show takes place. The Mayor goes to Westminster and there, but not within the City itself, he swears allegiance to the sovereign in the presence of the judges of the High Court. Lord Mayors of London are unique in terms of the power they wield. They have been elected since 1215, during the reign of King John. Their existence represented one of the provisions within Magna Carta, a document supervised and probably even written by the Knights Templar.

No monarch of Britain enters the City, at least in a ceremonial sense, until the Lord Mayor meets him or her at the Temple Bar (where the Templar headquarters in London used to be). The Lord Mayor presents the monarch with the sword of state and then he or she follows the Lord Mayor into the City.

The Corporation of London is older than Parliament itself and is unique as a governing body in Britain. It does elect its own representatives but not along party political lines. Its elections are based on a mixture of economic factors and tradition. Although the Corporation of the City does the same sort of jobs as those done elsewhere in Britain (refuse collection, sewage, housing, education, social services, etc) in other ways it is very different. It has its own police force, quite distinct from the Metropolitan Police, and it also runs the nation's Central Criminal Court at the Old Bailey.

Most of the major financial transactions of Britain take place within the City of London. Beyond this the City's institutions are responsible for many hundreds of billions of pounds of business from abroad. All of these transactions are administered and governed by this unique "State within a State" and much of what the City does lies beyond the scope of Parliament to influence it in a day-to-day sense. Most of what takes place within the City in a financial sense also falls under the influence of the Bank of England, which is located within the boundaries of the old City.

The Bank of England was set up in 1694 during the reign of King William and Queen Mary. It was proposed by a London businessman, William Patterson, that an amount of £1,200,000 should be loaned to the government by the leading financiers of the City of London. In return the subscribers would be incorporated as the Governor and Company of the Bank of England.

As time went by the Bank moved to Threadneedle Street where it still remains today. The debt owed by the government to the Bank has grown and grown since its incorporation and in 1946 the Bank was nationalized. It remains the chief source of advice to the Treasury, which in turn tells the Chancellor of the Exchequer what money is available to him. Since 1997 the Bank has had full authority to set interest rates in order to achieve the government's chosen target for inflation.

The City of London was and remains a heavily Freemasonic institution. After the Great Fire, which destroyed much of the City in 1666, London as we see it today was planned, rebuilt, and administered by men who were almost all Freemasons. It is within the City that "the Crown" resides. This is an institution that is quite separate from the monarch. In the days of empire many of the States that fell under the sway of Great Britain were administered by the Crown and not by the British government. They were effectively under the overall control of the Mayor and Corporation of London and Freemasonic membership was a virtual prerequisite throughout much of the nineteenth and twentieth centuries. Lodges existed to serve the various functionaries of the City, for example the Bank of England had its own

Lodge, as did the various Inns of Court.

Also within the City of London are to be found these "Inns of Court." Barristers must be trained and elected through one of the four institutions. These are the Inner Temple, the Middle Temple, Gray's Inn, and Lincoln's Inn. Varying in the date of their creation between 1310 and 1357, the Inns of Court stand at the heart of the British judicial system. All the Inns of Court developed from buildings where "apprentice" lawyers gathered and were trained by their masters, forming what were very much like medieval guilds.

The Inns of Court are not "incorporated" and have their own systems of election. Meetings at the Inns of Court are known as "Parliaments." The leader in each case is known as "Master of the Bench" and he is elected mainly from among the members of his Inn, but can also come from among senior members of the judiciary.

The Inner Temple and the Middle Temple occupy buildings on the site where the London Headquarters of the Knights Templar used to be and they originated very shortly after the fourteenth-century attacks that were made on the Templars. The insignia of the Middle Temple not only reflects its location but also a direct association with the Knights Templar.

The insignia of the Middle Temple, carrying the red cross and Agnus Dei of the Knights Templar

Like the City of London itself, the formation of the Inns of Court and the importance of British law originated in the signing of Magna Carta, which, as I have observed, was overseen and probably written by the Templars.

Also to be found within the area occupied by the Inner and Middle Temples is the original church built by the Templars in 1240. Being what is termed a "Royal Peculiar" the Templar Church stands outside the usual episcopal control. It serves as a place of worship for the two Inns of Court, where those attending services can still look upon the stone effigies of long-dead Templar Masters. These, despite the accusations leveled at the Templars, have remained undamaged through the vicissitudes of English religious history.

There is no doubting the Templar and Masonic influences that together helped to create what is still one of the most important economic and political capital cities in the world. At the heart of it lies the British legal system, a model for many others across the planet. Also secure within the inviolate walls of London is the Bank of England, which holds to its heart as its emblem the image of Britannia – Goddess of Britain.

CHAPTER SEVENTEEN

AN EPILOGUE TO A VISION

AN EPILOGUE TO A VISION

My point of departure for this book was in trying to establish whether the vision of the Virgin Mary, reportedly seen by two urchin children in France in 1846, was genuine, whether it was a fabrication on the part of the witnesses, or whether it was an elaborately staged hoax.

One of my first observations, apart from taking note of the testimony of the children themselves, was the nature of the sky and the calendar at the time of the supposed apparition. No fewer than five planets were occupying the zodiac sign of Virgo, and Venus was a bright and distinct morning star at the time. There was virtually no moon to obscure the piercing face of Venus as it would have risen early on that morning. At the same time the vision appeared on the eve of the Feast of Our Lady of Sorrows and took place at a time when it was virtually certain that an account of it would become public "before" the Church authorities could do anything to quell it.

Identical astronomical patterns have attended important Freemasonic events, such as the laying of the cornerstone of the Capitol Building in Washington. I went on to discover that that same pattern existed on the day of the signing of the United States Constitution. It cannot be denied that by far the majority of those taking part were practicing Freemasons or that this would be seen as the most momentous moment for a new nation.

I knew there was a persistent rumor in France that the La Salette vision might have been deliberately "staged" and that it was widely considered that the culprits were Freemasons. This would make sense in one way because Freemasons in mid-nineteenth-century France were doing all that they could to heap scorn on the Roman Catholic Church. It was part of a war that was being fought ferociously on both sides. Republican sentiment in France was still strong and Masons of the Grand Orient de France were seeking a settled and ordered republic, free from the incursions of either a king or of Rome.

The vision of La Salette would prove to be a distinct embarrassment to the Vatican because of what the Virgin Mary had to say about members of the clergy.

The priests, ministers of my Son, the priests, by their bad life, by their irreverences and their impiety in celebrating the holy mysteries, by love of money, love of honor and of pleasures, the priests have become cesspools of impurity.

French Masons, in their ongoing war against the Vatican, would have been delighted by this slur against those who were running the Catholic Church, especially coming from the mouth of one of its most revered characters, the Virgin Mary. In addition the "Alta Vendita" had been published in the very same year of 1846. This had supposedly been a firsthand account of a Masonic plot to infiltrate and eventually to destroy the Catholic Church.

As regards the actual nature of the vision I can find nothing within it that could not have been staged, using only the technology of the day, together with the incredulity of two uneducated children who led drab and colorless lives. The bright light associated with the vision could have been created using "limelight." Limelight had first been created in 1825 by two separate Englishmen. These were Thomas Drummond and Goldsworthy Gurney. It involved burning calcium oxide (lime) in a hot hydrogen flame and was used regularly in theatres and music halls at the time as stage lighting. Limelight is extremely bright, even in the full glare of day. Mary both appeared from and disappeared back into a bright light. Melanie even suggested that Mary had disappeared into the light because she didn't want them (the children) to know where she had gone. Even very simple pyrotechnics could have supplied an event that would have fooled Melanie and Maximin.

By their own admission both children had been asleep before the Virgin Mary appeared, leaving ample time for whatever was necessary to be put in place. Even without limelight or fireworks, which would have necessitated some equipment, a little stage subterfuge of some sort would surely have impressed the children. The "apparition" they saw before them was certainly way beyond their ordinary experience. It is known that the vision took place on a glorious day, with the blazing sun beginning to drop toward the West. This, in itself, might have provided the means of appearance and departure the actress needed.

The elaborate and colorful costume, with its roses, jewels, and adornments would not have been hard to create and would have been certain to strike a sense of awe into both Maximin and Melanie, who would never have seen anything like it in the grubby back streets of Corps. Taken together with the sheer "incredulity" of seeing such a figure on a remote mountainside, it would seem likely that the children would be easily fooled into thinking the figure had a supernatural origin. Even then there might have been a slight hint of "ordinary" because Maximin in particular tried at first tried to attribute a natural origin to the beautiful woman. He thought she might be a housewife who had run away from home.

One major "proof" of the validity of Mary's appearance, according to many believers, is the fact that she appeared to know things about the children that no earthly agency could have known. Actually, this amounts to very little. Mary reminded Maximin of an incident that had taken place at the time the corn should have been ready for harvest in the previous year. The lad had been walking with his father when they had chanced upon a farmer, lamenting the spoiled nature of his wheat.

This in itself means little or nothing. Maximin's father was, at the time, a heavy drinker in the bars of Corps. Anyone could have bought him a pastis and sat with him for a friendly chat, extricating the necessary information and passing it on to the actress who would play the part of the Virgin.

Most damning of all are the prophecies given to both children by Mary at La Salette. Most of them relate to the period immediately after the La Salette vision itself and to political and religious struggles taking place during that part of the nineteenth century. Where these messages are not ambiguously apocalyptic, they can be shown to be widely inaccurate. For example,

> In the year 1864, Lucifer with a great number of demons will be unleashed from hell; they will abolish the faith little by little and even in persons consecrated to God; they will blind them in such a way that barring a particular grace these persons will take on the spirit of these bad angels: several religious houses will lose the faith entirely and will lose many souls.

No event from the period seems to bear out this prophecy. Later in Melanie's message we find:

> In the year 1865, the abomination will be seen in holy places; in convents, the flowers of the Church will be decayed and the demon will make himself as the king of hearts. May those who are at the head of religious communities keep themselves on guard for persons whom they must receive, because the demon will use of all his malice in order to introduce into religious Orders persons devoted to sin, for disorders and the love of carnal pleasures will be spread by all the earth.

One again I can find no event in French or world history that bears out this prophesy.

In Maximin's message we are told:

A great country, now Protestant, in the north of Europe, will be converted; by the support of this country all the other nations of the world will be converted.

These events, we are told "will arrive in the other century, at the latest in the year two thousand." The year at the time of writing this book is 2005 and nothing of the sort outlined here has yet taken place.

While it might be acceptable to believe that the strange planetary alignment that occurred on the day of the La Salette vision does not mitigate a genuine supernatural happening, one would expect a true vision of the Blessed Virgin Mary not to be confused, or even absolutely wrong, with regard to future events.

With nothing about the vision beyond human resource and ingenuity, we might say that the case is more or less proven and that it must have been a hoax, though we could not directly blame Freemasons for the supposed apparition because nobody ever admitted responsibility. Nor is this really the end of the story. While it is certain that French Freemasons at the time wanted to discredit Catholic priests and the Church generally, it might seem strange that they would do so in such a way that would bring even greater reverence to one of Catholicism's central characters – the Virgin Mary. In the end they would have been guilty of shooting themselves in the foot because La Salette is still visited by thousands of pilgrims every year – most of them fervent Catholics. What is more, though the protagonists could not have realized it at the time, the slightly less than complimentary message of La Salette, with regard to the Church, was superseded by the much more satisfactory appearance of Mary at Lourdes.

If we are going to see Freemasons as the promoters of a hoax at La Salette, it is surely the case that discrediting the orthodox Catholic Church can only have been "part" of their raison d'etre. What is more, the perpetrators left definite "clues" as to their arcane religious and astronomical leanings and knowledge. The vision took place at the very time of year that the Mystery rites of Demeter had been practiced in Ancient Greece – a fact that the La Salette vision had in common with the American Masonic ceremonies.

Such a perfect astronomical pattern as occurred that day at La Salette is very rare indeed. It is true that on that particular date in September the sun will always occupy the zodiac sign of Virgo. But to also find the moon, Mercury, Venus, and Mars in the same zodiac sign is most uncommon, especially when one considers that the moon was only one day away from its darkest and also bearing in mind the religious significance of the day – the eve of the Feast of Our Lady of Sorrows.

Much of the dialogue that took place between the children and the Virgin was associated with the harvest and specifically with wheat. Sheaves of wheat were an enduring symbol of the Goddess of old. This fact was replete with symbolism because the dying and reborn God, to whom she was at one and the same time mother and wife, was representative of the yearly harvest – sacrificed each year by the sickle, so that its grain could be replanted and grow again the following year.

In pictures representing the zodiac sign of Virgo, the Virgin is almost always shown carrying two sheaves of wheat. This is also true of the Greek Goddess Demeter, and her Roman counterpart, Ceres, from whom the word "cereal" for grain crops is derived. The connection between these ancient deities and the Virgin Mary is prominent and obvious. In Troyes Cathedral, Champagne, France, for example, there is a beautiful statue of the Virgin Mary who carries a sheaf of wheat cradled in one arm and loaves of bread in her other hand.

The most likely individuals to have carried out the La Salette hoax were people who did have an interest in discrediting the leadership of the orthodox Catholic Church, but who also had their own religious imperatives. That they left a deliberate message of what those imperatives were there is no doubt. It simply requires someone with an understanding of astronomy, astrology, and ancient mythology to read it.

The association between the astronomical patterns at La Salette and those in the infant United States cannot be ignored. In the case of the cornerstone ceremony and the signing of the American Constitution, we know that Freemasons were involved. I have also demonstrated how important the zodiac sign of Virgo has been to Freemasonry, together with a prominently placed Venus, appearing as a morning star. It seems highly likely then that if the La Salette vision was a hoax, Freemasonic influence lay behind its staging. But the people involved were almost certainly more than run-of-the-mill members of some local Lodge – this much is displayed by their astronomical and mythological knowledge.

For many years now it has seemed evident to me that there was, and almost certainly still is, a significant group of people in the world who "apparently" follow the doctrines of the established Church, but who, in reality, have their own slant on orthodoxy. I have previously described these people as being like mistletoe growing on the tree of the Christian faith. In other words, they have their own unique and ancient beliefs, though in the main they are quite happy to maintain these in secret, most likely within closed family groups.

These are precisely the people the author and Freemason Anthony Trollope was pointing at when he described Mr. Thorne and people like him:

> They were, and felt themselves to be, the only true depositories left of certain Eleusinian Mysteries, of certain deep and wondrous services of worship by which alone the gods could be rightly approached. To them and them only was it now given to know these things, and to perpetuate them, if that might still be done, by the careful and secret education of their children.

He went on to say:

> We have read how private and peculiar forms of worship have been carried on from age to age in families, which to the outer world have apparently adhered to the services of some ordinary church.

Let us imagine for a moment, that within orthodox Catholicism, we represent part of a group of people who accept "the trappings" of Catholicism, but not all of its doctrines. We retain a reverence for the Great Goddess of ancient times and we see in the story of Jesus a "recent" manifestation of the Goddess, Young God, and Old God trilogy that was once pre-eminent across most of Europe and Asia. Now we should look inside an average Catholic church. We can see the Virgin Mary, crowned as the Queen of Heaven and sanctified as the Mother of God. We can also look at the crucifix, displaying the dying corn God, sacrificed, as was the case with Osiris and Dionysus. Even within the most sacred rite of the Church, the sacrament, we observe how well this place and this form of worship suits our purposes.

Jesus used the analogy, and it is repeated every time the sacrament is taken, of his blood being wine and his body being bread. His words directly echo our own feelings about the "true" nature of Christianity. To us he "is" the dying and reborn corn god of old.

As worshipers we exist "in" but not "of" the Church and yet, like Mr. Thorne, we remain content in the knowledge that ours is the "true" faith – the genuine mystery that only the elect can know.

Only when shifting Church dogma threatens to isolate us from the "source" of that mystery will we move to take action. Those who went before us have gone to immense trouble to maintain the "church within a church" that allows our "peculiar forms of worship" to be maintained, generation after generation. Working from within organizations such as the Cistercians, the Knights Templar, and Freemasonry, society and in particular religion, have been influenced to suit our beliefs and our needs. We are patient people, we always have been. And like Mr. Thorne we are:

> not without a certain pleasure that such knowledge, though given to us, should be debarred from the multitude.

For at least a thousand years, but most likely for very much longer, we and our kind have gone to great trouble to gradually mould society to suit our ends. Our beliefs are not simply religious, we also have a social and even a political imperative. We believe absolutely in democracy, free speech, and personal freedom. We maintain our strong religious convictions but we also look towards that "New Jerusalem" – to a world in which all men and women are genuinely equal. We are not evangelists and do not seek converts – that is simply not our way, but whether others would consider our point of view right or wrong, we patiently maintain our influence and wait for society to catch up. It doesn't matter how long this might take – we are content to wait.

To some this will sound like nonsense but over two decades of research has taught me to recognize "the golden thread" that weaves in and out of the tapestry of time. It cannot be said that "Freemasonry" is responsible for these beliefs because they predate the Craft. In any case, very few Freemasons are party to them. Like other groups such as the Knights Templar, Freemasonry has acted as a "conduit." This unique group of movers and shakers certainly created Freemasonry but it has no need to control it in a day-by-day sense. Freemasonry is imbued with a particular set of social, political, and even religious beliefs and it has had a tremendous part to play in the building of the world we see today. But those who created the Craft know that it can either be used or left to its own devices, according to the needs of the moment.

The numbers in this shadowy group may be relatively small, but its influence has been out of all proportion. It constantly puts itself into the right positions to give society a "nudge" here and a "prod" there. It remains generally invisible by adopting the tactic of "hiding in plain view," but it carries, at its heart, the greatest secret ever shared by a small section of humanity.

When its interests or its vision of the future is threatened it can act as an *agent provocateur*, as may well have been the case with the La Salette vision. In particular, it desires to keep the feminine principle within Christianity central and recognizable. Those ruling the Catholic Church fight back. They know they have opponents because they have felt their influence for centuries but they cannot identify their enemies because, as with the notions of the Alta Vendita, members of this secret congregation exist at all levels of society and religion. To the Roman Catholic Church this is the enemy within, sensed but not identifiable.

This is the group of people, often identified as the "illuminati" that, it is suggested, is intent upon creating a New World Order. This cannot be denied, except for the fact that there is nothing new about it at all. Since at least the time of the deliberate strategy of a few influential families in Burgundy and Champagne in the eleventh century to destroy both feudal Church and State, the New World Order has been coming.

By promoting international trade and subverting the power of the Church from within, this group of families re-drew the map of Europe and ultimately that of the world. The religious belief that underpins the strategy is probably as old as humanity itself and it simply refuses to go away.

The average Freemason, meeting on any night of the week in any one of thousands of Lodges across the face of the planet, is no more aware of these facts than was a humble choir monk in Melrose Abbey or a Templar warrior baking under his armor in the desert of Sinai. He knows little or nothing of his supposed Satanic practices, of the confusion between Lucifer and the devil or of the Eleusian Mystery in which he has actually taken part. He is simply one member of a huge fraternity, which as far as he is concerned is given over to raising money for charity, while at the same time allowing him to mix amiably with like-minded individuals.

But someone knows. There was nothing arbitrary about the position of the sun, moon, and planets on that day at La Salette in 1846, nor when the first stone of the Capitol building was laid so that the infant United States could have a hope for its "daring plan" of self-rule. Nor should we be in any doubt that the Statue of Liberty is and was meant to be the largest statue of the Goddess that has ever been constructed. And "someone" very carefully planned the time and the day on which the American Constitution would be signed – the most important symbolic act in the creation of a nation.

In all probability we will never know the absolute truth behind the apparition of La Salette and it is extremely unlikely that we will ever be able to identify the actual culprits. Of course, for some it will remain what it appeared to be – a genuine visitation of the Blessed Virgin Mary to two small and deprived children on a French mountain. After all, if the visitation was supernatural, it would not have been difficult for God to choose the right astronomical patterns to further "prove" its validity. But this does nothing to explain the similar astronomical patterns that definitely are associated with Freemasonry.

The dispute between Roman Catholicism, together with Christian fundamentalism, and Freemasonry will continue. At the moment Freemasonry seems to be somewhat on the back foot, probably because leading politicians both in Britain and the United States have their own religious imperatives and also because they sense a groundswell of suspicion regarding the Craft on the part of voters. Those who run Freemasonry do all they can to avoid courting controversy. This might be understandable but it is also unfortunate because it belittles and hides something ancient and fundamental at the heart of the Craft.

I know from the personal contacts I have made that "Mr. Thorne"s do still exist, both inside the Church and within Freemasonry. It is unlikely that after a thousand years or more they would stand up and admit to the fact in any public forum. They don't need to because the evidence is all around us. It lies in the history of our societies – in the overthrow of feudalism and the rise of free enterprise and capitalism. The continued reverence for the Goddess, whatever she is called today, can be seen in any Catholic Church and also within the establishments of the High Church of England. Her image adorns coins and bank notes produced by many countries and she remains the enduring symbol of France, the United States, and Great Britain. In truth she is almost everywhere we look and her form is so common that we fail to recognize either its presence or its significance. Even when she actually bears one of the ancient names of the Goddess and stands 305 feet tall, as is the case with the Statue of Liberty, we still don't understand.

Nobody, not even Freemasonry with its strange practices and arcane beliefs, has to fight hard to reinstate the Goddess – she never went away.

APPENDIX ONE

THE ASTROLOGICAL CHARTS

I have included the three most significant astrological charts mentioned in the body of the book, mainly for the sake of those readers who already have some understanding of astronomy and/or astrology. However, since other readers will also doubtless be interested in this aspect of my research I am also including a brief explanation of what the charts mean.

It is important to reiterate that it is not necessary for readers to in any way accept the premise that the position of the stars and planets at any given point in time has a bearing on the lives of people living on the Earth. The issue at stake is whether other people, at significant times in our history, have accepted the validity of astrology.

It seems quite evident to me that specific dates were deliberately chosen on a number of occasions and for important ceremonies of a Freemasonic nature. This is particularly evident during the 18th and 19th centuries. I would include amongst these significant dates the Apparition of the Virgin Mary at La Salette, France, in 1846. In terms of mythology and historical practice, this incident showed an astrological pattern on the day and at the time of day at which the event took place that is in absolute accordance with what took place on that lonely mountain. The possibility of those events happening by chance at the same time as the Sun, Moon and planets were arranged in this way is beyond credibility. As a result only two possible explanations spring to mind. Either divine intervention is a reality or whoever stage-managed the apparition deliberately chose the time and day in question.

Similar patterns are evident in the case of the signing of the American Constitution and the laying of the Cornerstone of the Capitol Building in Washington DC. In each case a date was chosen at which time the Sun occupied the zodiac sign of Virgo. In addition, Venus was always a bright and significant Morning Star, rising ahead of the Sun on the days in question. In all three cases the events also took place during the crucial week that had been set aside for the celebration of the Demeter Mysteries in Eleusis, Greece.

An astrological chart of the sort that follows is nothing more or less than a map of the sky. The outer wheel or bezel represents the divisions of the sky known as the signs of the zodiac. The zodiac signs each represent $1/12^{th}$ of the plane of the ecliptic, that band of the sky in which the Sun, Moon and planets can be observed to travel. Each of the zodiac signs is represented by a glyph. These are as follows:

♈	**Aries**
♉	**Taurus**
♊	**Gemini**
♋	**Cancer**
♌	**Leo**
♍	**Virgo**
♎	**Libra**
♏	**Scorpio**
♐	**Sagittarius**
♑	**Capricorn**
♒	**Aquarius**
♓	**Pisces**

The Sun, as viewed from Earth, appears to pass through each of the zodiac signs in turn, remaining about a month in each. It is during the late Summer and early Autumn in the Northern hemisphere that the Sun occupies the zodiac sign of Virgo - from around August 23rd to September 22nd

A zodiac chart is set to a particular time of day. The zodiac sign on the extreme left of each chart is that sign that was appearing over the Eastern horizon at the time of day in question.

On the inner part of the chart wheels are displayed the symbols that refer to the Sun, Moon and planets. These are as follows:

☉	**Sun**
☽	**Moon**
☿	**Mercury**
♀	**Venus**
♂	**Mars**
♃	**Jupiter**
♄	**Saturn**
♅	**Uranus**
♆	**Neptune**
♇	**Pluto**

Beside each heavenly body can be found a number, for example 16°. This represents the number of decrees of arc within any given zodiac sign occupied by a particular body at the time for which the chart was operative.

A typical astrological chart contains much more information than is shown in the charts that follow but I have deliberately chosen to keep these simple so as not to confuse readers who are unfamiliar with the symbols and terminology of astrology.

LA Salette France
Sepember 19th 1846 1pm

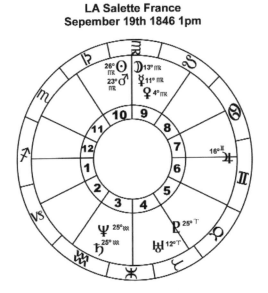

Simplified astrological chart showing the position
of the planets on Sept 19th 1846 at 1pm
La Salette vision of the Virgin Mary

**Signing of American Constitution
September 17th 1787 Midday**

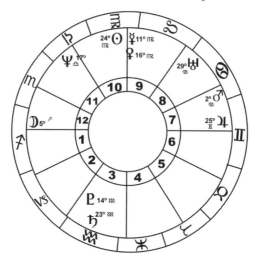

**Simplified astrological chart showing the position
of the planets on Sept 17th 1787 at Midday
Signing of American Constitution Philadelphia**

**The Laying of the Cornerstone, Capitol Building
September 18th 1793 10am**

**Simplified astrological chart showing the position
of the planets on Sept 18th 1793 at 10am
Laying of the Cornerstone, Capitol Building
Washington DC**

INDEX

A

33rd degree Mason 33
Ablandins 2, 6, 7, 10, 28
Academy of Science, France 103-106
Adams, John 110
Agrippa, Heinrich Cornelius 145
Alta Vendita 130-141, 162, 175, 181
Anatolia viii, 50, 53
Anne, Queen 37, 104
Antoninus Pius, Emperor 163-165
Arianism 53
Ark of the Covenant 69
Ashmole, Elias 102
Asia vii, 179
astrology/astrological 25-30, 39, 43, 48, 101, 114, 139, 178
Atbash 90, 91, 157
Athens 46, 47, 114, 117, 125
Aubrey, John 102
Augustine of Hippo 61

B

Baphomet 76, 91, 157
Barney Ritual 44
Bartholdi, Frederic Auguste 112
Baudoin II 68,
Bayle 110
Benedict of Nursia, Saint 61
Benedict XII, Pope 75
Benedict XVI, Pope 142-3
Benedictine 62, 63, 79, 80, 94, 95
Bernard of Clairveaux 62-74, 79, 93, 94, 134, 136, 137
Bernard of Thiron 79
Bonapart, Napoleon 103, 124, 125
Boniface VIII, Pope 75
Book of Revelations 61, 66
Borda 104

Boston Tea Party 109, 111
Bridget 90, 92, 164
Brigantia 164
Britannia 104, 163-167, 171
British Government 109, 114, 125, 169
Brittany 24
de Bruillard, Bishop 12, 13
Burgundy 57, 58, 60, 62, 66, 127, 133, 181
Byblos 45

C

Calvet, Melanie 2-14, 21, 27, 29, 136-139, 175, 176
Calvin, John 96
Capitalism viii, ix, 182
Capitol Building, USA 115- 118, 139, 174, 181
Carbonari, the 130, 131
Carolingian 57, 58, 92
Catholic Church viii, 11, 21, 29, 30, 35, 56, 57, 72, 76, 78, 84, 85, 88, 94, 95, 103-105, 108, 122, 124, 127, 139, 140, 142, 143, 174, 175, 177, 178, 181
Catholic/ism x, 21, 27, 29, 34, 36, 37, 58, 63, 66, 80, 85, 88, 89, 91, 92, 94-97, 101, 104-106, 108, 127, 130-132, 134-137, 140, 142, 143, 162, 177, 179, 182
Ceres 126, 178
Champagne 57, 58, 60-63, 66, 68-70, 72, 74-76, 79, 123, 127, 133, 134, 178, 181
Charbonnerie démocratique 131,
Charlemagne 57, 58, 123
Charles I, King 36, 37. 100
Charles II, King 37, 102, 104, 163, 165

Charpentier 93
Chartres 73, 93
Châtillon-sur Marne 60
choir monks 63, 35, 181
Christian Church viii, x, 54, 89, 90, 96, 140, 156
Christian/ity viii, ix, x, 6. 34, 35, 45, 46, 53—61, 68, 71, 73, 74, 82, 88, 90-95, 120-122, 125, 126, 131, 140, 142, 178, 179, 181, 182
Cistercian 62-66, 69, 79, 85, 91, 94, 95, 106, 123, 127, 133, 136, 180
Citeaux 62, 63
City, the viii
Clement V, Pope 75
Clement XII, Pope 105
Clermont 60
Clovis 55-57, 92
Consalvi, Cardinal 131
Constantine 52-55, 92, 147
Corn God 48, 49, 55, 83, 179
Corteville, Michael Fr. 14
Craft, the 32-35, 38, 42, 43, 80, 101, 103, 105, 108, 110, 114, 122, 123, 131, 142, 143, 150, 152, 154, 157, 160, 180, 182
Crete 47-49, 90
Cromwell, Oliver 36, 37, 102
Cross, Jeremy 44
Crusade 60, 62, 71, 132, 133
Culdee/Culdean 56, 66, 80, 85, 94
da Vinci, Leonardo 145

D

Dafoe, Stephen 76
Dagobert I I 56
Dee, John 101
Demeter 45-49, 55, 57, 90, 111, 114, 118, 126, 146, 162, 164, 166, 177, 178
Democracy viii, ix, 63, 79, 125, 163, 168, 180
Descartes 110
Diderot 110
Dinas 78
Dionysus 46-49, 118, 179

Druid 38, 56, 92
Dyer, Colin 150

E

Earth vii, 15-20, 24-28, 105, 117, 118, 144, 148-150
East Indian Tea Company 109
Egypt vii, 27, 45, 48, 52, 54, 111, 144, 164
Eiffel, Gustav 112
Eleusis 47, 114, 117, 118, 161
Elizabeth I, Queen 101, 115, 165
Essene 57, 61, 62, 64, 65, 69, 90, 134

F

Father Time 43, 44, 48
Fatima 29
Fellowcraft 38
Feminine x, 28, 90, 157, 164, 181
Feronia 111
Feudalism ix, 57, 79, 104, 134, 182
France x, 2, 8, 11, 17, 20, 21, 24, 25, 29, 34, 35, 37, 55-60, 70-80, 84, 93, 100, 103, 104, 106, 110-113, 122-127, 130-137, 162, 163, 165, 174, 178, 182
Franklin, Benjamin 103, 121, 122, 123
Freemason/ry x, 22, 25, 30, 32-40, 42-45, 48-50, 58, 73, 74, 76, 78-85, 100-106, 108-118, 121-125, 130, 131, 142, 143, 147, 150, 152, 154, 156, 157, 16169, 174, 177-182
Freemason: Scottish Rite 37, 160
Freemason:York Rite 37
French Revolution 8, 103, 104, 111, 112, 123, 124, 127, 131, 162

G

Galileo 105
George I, King 37, 104
Giraud Maximin 2-13, 20, 27, 138, 139, 175, 176
Gnostic 47, 100
Goddess x, 28, 29, 45-49, 55, 88, 90-93, 101, 111, 114, 124-127, 135, 144,

146, 147, 154-157, 160, 163, 164, 167, 171, 178-182
Godfroi du Bouillon   62
Golden Mean,the   144
Got, Bertrand de   75
Grand Lodge   32, 37, 38, 100, 108, 109, 150
Great Architect of the Universe   34
Great Pyramid   vii
Greece/Greek   45-47, 52-57, 79, 90, 115, 118, 121, 125, 144-147, 150, 156, 161-165, 177, 178
Green Man   82, 83
Gregory the Great, Pope   60
Gregory XVI, Pope   130, 134
Gresham, Thomas   101, 102
Guichard, Xavier   24, 25
Guild   32, 33, 38, 74, 84, 151, 170

H

Hades   46, 118
Hadrian II, Pope   57
Hanovarian   108
Hebrew   18, 43, 55
Henry III, King   75
Henry Vlll, King   36
Hewitt Brown, Robert   39
Hiram Abif   38, 43, 44, 48, 49
Hiram of Tyre   43
Holy Land   viii, 60, 62, 71, 74, 75
Holy City   70
Honorius II, Pope   70, 71
Horus   45

I

Immaculate Conception   30. 136-140
Inanna   118
Innocent II, Pope   71
Innocent III, Pope   72
Invisible College, the   101, 102
Ishtar   90, 118
Isis   45-49, 52, 55, 90, 93, 111, 164
Israel   69, 89
Italy   15, 17, 21, 52, 57, 65, 78, 79, 94, 130, 131, 133

J

James I, King36, 37, 85
James II, King   37, 104, 105, 162
James IV, King   85
Jefferson, Thomas   122
Jesus   4, 16-19, 27, 53-57, 61, 84, 88-91, 94, 95, 131, 134-138, 179
Jew/ish   57, 66, 69, 73, 121, 134, 147
John, King   72, 168
John the Baptist   61, 80
John XXII, Pope   78
John Paul ll, Pope   142
Junior Warden   33
Jupiter   144

K

Kabbalah/Kabbalistic   73
Knight, Christopher   24, 25, 68, 83
Knights Hospitaller   78
Knights of Christ   70, 78
Knights Templar   66, 68-75, 78-84, 127, 134, 136, 150, 151, 157, 167, 168, 170, 180
Knossos   90
Krater   146

L

La Rochelle   76, 84
Lafayette, Marquis de   152
Lagrange   104
Laplace   104
Laurentin, René Fr.   14
Lawrence, Commodore   44
lay brothers   63, 64
Leo X, Pope   94, 95, 134
Levant   62, 68, 71-74
Levi Eliphas   154-156
Liberty   101, 111-113, 124-126, 131, 152, 154, 167, 181, 182
Locke, John   102
Lomas Robert   68, 83
Lombard   57
Louis XVI, King of France   123
Lourdes   13, 21, 29, 30, 135, 136, 138-140, 177

Lucifer   15, 155, 156, 176, 181
Lucy/Lucia, Saint   156
Luther, Martin   95, 96

M
Madison, James   121
Magna Carta   72, 168, 170
Malta   88
Margaret, Queen   80
Marianne   125-127, 135, 163, 167
Mars   28, 144, 178
Massabielle   135
Master Mason   33, 38, 40
Mayne, Michael   162
Megalithic   24, 25
Megalthic yard   24
Mélin, Fr.   11, 12
Melrose Abbey   79, 181
Mercury   28, 114, 117, 144, 178
Merovingian   55-58, 62
Minoan   47, 49, 90, 125
Mithra/ism   52-54, 147, 164
Molay, Jaques de   78
Molesmes,Robert de   62
Monge   104
Montesquieu
Moon19, 24, 26-28, 45, 82, 114, 149, 174, 178, 181
Moray, Robert   100-102
Moses   69, 73
Mother Lodge   85
Mother of God   89, 90, 92, 96, 135, 179
Muslim   35, 60, 61

N
Napoleon   15, 103, 124, 125, 162
New York   viii, 44, 112, 113
Newton, Isaac   104-106, 123
Nicea   53-55, 91

O
Odo of Lagery   60
Ogive   73, 151

Osiris   45, 48, 49, 179
Our Lady of Sorrows   27, 28, 49, 174, 178
Oxford Movement   162

P
Pacca, Cardinal   131
Paine, Thomas   110, 120, 121, 162
Palestine   53, 57, 61, 65, 68, 69, 71, 134, 136, 140
Pascal   110
Payan, Hugh de   62, 68, 70, 71, 81
Payramale, Dean   138
Pentacle   73, 143-158
Pentateuch   147
Pentemychos   146
Pepin the Short   56, 57
Persephone   45, 46, 111, 118, 146
Phaleron   47
Phi   144, 145, 149, 152
Philip IV of France   75, 76, 81
Phoenician   43, 45
Pius IX, Pope   15, 137
Pius XII, Pope   140
Planet/ary   24, 26-29, 114, 139, 144, 149, 174, 177, 181
Pluto   46
Pra, Baptiste   3-11
Puritans   163
Pyramid   viii, 57
Pythagoras   144, 146

Q
Queen of Heaven   88-90, 93. 140, 144, 179
Qumran   61, 64, 69

R
Raleigh, Walter   101
Ratzinger, Cardinal   142, 143
Rievaulx Abbey   64, 65
Revere, Paul   110, 111

Rheims   93,
Richelieu, Cardinal   100
Robert the Bruce   79

Roettier, Philip   165
Roman Empire   52, 53, 91, 93, 164
Rome   13, 15, 19, 20, 36, 37, 55-58, 61, 75, 78, 92, 97, 111, 115, 127, 135-137, 140, 162, 174
Rose   135, 138, 147-149
Rosemerta   93
Rosicrucian   100
Rosslyn   80-84, 151
Rousseau   110, 124
Royal Society, the   100-106, 165

S

Saladin   74
Salian Franks   55
salt   25
Satan   35, 156
Saturn   144
Schaw, William   84
Schonfield, Hugh   90, 91
Scotland   24, 36, 65, 74, 79-81, 85, 151
Selme, Pierre 2-8
Set   45
Sinai   69, 181
Sinclair, William   81-84
Solomon   43, 44, 66, 94, 147, 150
Solomon, Seal of   147, 150
Solomon, temple of   33, 38, 43, 68, 70, 83, 84, 105
Sophia   90, 91, 93, 157
Soubirous, Bernadette, Saint   13, 135, 138, 139
South America   viii, 92
St Clair sur Ept   81
St. Andrews Lodge   109
Statue of Liberty 112, 113, 181, 182
Stephen Harding   62
Sumerian   118, 144, 149
Sun   26-28, 46, 48, 68, 82, 105, 114, 117, 118, 148, 149, 156, 177, 181

T

Talleyrand   103, 104
Tartraros   146

Theobald, Saint   130
Theotokus   55, 91
Thibaud II   70
Third degree   38, 40, 42-44, 48, 49, 130, 131, 150, 152, 165
Thom, Alexander   24
Tironian Monks   85
Trollope, Anthony   160-163, 179
Troyes   55, 60, 62, 63, 66, 68, 69-71, 73, 76, 81, 93, 123, 178

U

United States Constitution   174
United States of America   viii, 39, 110-112, 114, 116, 118, 120-122, 152, 157, 161, 178. 181, 182
Urban II, Pope   60, 132

V

Vatican   13, 14, 21, 29, 30, 57, 60, 72, 75, 79, 85, 94, 95, 97, 105, 127, 131, 134-137, 140, 142, 143, 174, 175
Venus   2, 3, 28, 114, 117, 118, 139, 144, 148-150, 154, 156, 174, 178
Victor III   60,
Virgin Mary   8, 10, 21, 24, 27-30, 49, 55, 65, 72, 80, 85, 88-90, 92-95, 101, 118, 126, 127, 134-140, 147, 160, 163, 164, 174, 175, 177-179
Virgo, zodiac sign of 27, 28, 39, 43, 46, 48, 114, 117, 118, 139, 146, 174, 178
Visitation, the   96
Voltaire   110, 123, 124, 131

W

Weeping Virgin, the   42-50
William of Orange   37, 104
Worshipful Master   33, 116
Wren, Christopher   102, 165

Z

Zeus   46, 125
Zodiac   26-28, 39, 43, 48, 149, 178
Zoroastrian/ism 52